Grammar Galaxy
Adventures in Language Arts

Red Star

Melanie Wilson, Ph.D.
Rebecca Mueller, Illustrator

GRAMMAR GALAXY: RED STAR
Copyright © 2019 by Fun to Learn Books

ISBN: 978-0-9965703-8-1

Table of Contents

Table of Contents...3

A Note to Teachers 5

A Note to Students 6

Prologue 7

Unit I: Adventures in Literature 8

Chapter 1: Theme...9

Chapter 2: Supporting Evidence 14

Chapter 3: Author Study 18

Chapter 4: Symbolism..23

Chapter 5: Foreshadowing 30

Chapter 6: Flashback..34

Chapter 7: Hyperbole...39

Chapter 8: Humor 45

Unit II: Adventures in Spelling & Vocabulary 50

Chapter 9: Overused Words..51

Chapter 10: Slang..56

Chapter 11: Word Analogies 62

Chapter 12: Prefixes, Suffixes & Root Words.......................67

Chapter 13: Apostrophes...72

Chapter 14: Hyphens...77

Chapter 15: Tricky Homophones...82

Chapter 16: Shades of Meaning...88

Chapter 17: Writing with Numbers.......................................94

Unit III: Adventures in Grammar 100

Chapter 18: Participles..101

Chapter 19: Objects of Prepositions.....................................105

Chapter 20: Subjective vs. Objective Pronouns....................110

Chapter 21: Interrogative Pronouns......................................115

Chapter 22: Demonstrative Pronouns 121

Chapter 23: Reflexive Pronouns 127

Chapter 24: Indefinite Pronouns 134

Chapter 25: Dependent vs. Independent Clauses................................139

Chapter 26: Colons & Semicolons...146

Unit IV: Adventures in Composition & Speaking................................151

Chapter 27: Business Letter 152

Chapter 28: Descriptive Writing 159

Chapter 29: Sentence Starters 165

Chapter 30: Writing with a Partner..169

Chapter 31: Creating Titles..174

Chapter 32: Advice Column 180

Chapter 33: Choosing a Research Paper Topic...................................185

Chapter 34: Note-Taking & Outlining 190

Chapter 35: Citing References 197

Chapter 36: Informative Speaking..202

About the Author 207

About the Illustrator...208

A Note to Teachers

I'm passionate about language arts. I love to read, write, and speak. As a homeschooling mom, I wanted my own children and my friends' children to share my passion. Over the years, I found aspects of many different curricula that clicked with my students. But I never found something that did everything I wanted a complete curriculum for elementary students to do:

- Use the most powerful medium to teach language arts: story
- Give the why of language arts to motivate students
- Teach to mastery rather than drill the same concepts year after year
- Limit seat work and use little-to-no-prep games to teach instead
- Teach all language arts: literature concepts, vocabulary, spelling, writing, and public speaking

I felt called to create my own fast, easy, and fun curriculum for homeschooling parents and others who want to see students succeed in language arts.

Grammar Galaxy: Red Star is for students who are at about a fifth-grade level or have completed Volumes 1-3 or their equivalent. *Red Star* can be read and completed independently if your student is at a 3rd grade reading level or above. The stories and concepts are appropriate for students in first through eighth grade, however, making this a perfect read-aloud for families. If you are reading to your student, be sure to point out the synonyms for vocabulary words that are provided. Following each story, there are questions to check for understanding. Students should complete the corresponding mission in the *Mission Manual* before moving on to the next story. The *Mission Manual* can be purchased at GrammarGalaxyBooks.com/shop.

My hope is that your student will accept the call to be a guardian of Grammar Galaxy.

Melanie Wilson

A Note to Students

I need your help. Grammar Galaxy is in trouble. The Gremlin is working hard to keep kids from reading, learning new words, and spelling correctly. He also wants to keep them from writing and public speaking. He knows that if he succeeds, the English language will be weak, and life will be miserable.

Here is how you can help defeat the Gremlin. First, read each chapter in the text, paying attention to the vocabulary words that are in **bold text**. Note the synonym (word with similar meaning) that is given for each. Then make sure you can answer the discussion questions at the end of each chapter. If you can't, review the text, and if you still need help, ask your teacher. Finally, complete the mission in your mission manual with the same number as the chapter in this book.

I'm proud to have you join us as a guardian of the galaxy!

Melanie Wilson

Prologue

The king of Grammar Galaxy tried not to worry. He had made his three children, Kirk, Luke, and Ellen English, guardians of the galaxy. Together with the other young guardians on planet English, they had defeated the Gremlin and saved the English language many, many times. Words and punctuation marks were returned to their planetary homes, destructive laws were changed, and the kids had learned a lot about literature, grammar, and writing.

But would the Gremlin's schemes finally get the best of them? Would they eventually face a crisis they couldn't overcome with the help of *The Guide to Grammar Galaxy*? He didn't know. He asked Screen for a status report on the galaxy. All seemed well for the moment.

Unit I: Adventures in Literature

Chapter 1

"I decided what we will be reading aloud as a family." The queen made this announcement as they were finishing dessert one evening.

"What is it? What is it?" the kids prodded her.

The king used his fork and knife to create a drum roll on the table. The queen chastised him. "You'll be sending crumbs everywhere doing that!"

"That's okay. Comet deserves dessert too," he said as the dog darted around his chair looking for leftovers. "Just tell us which book we will be reading," he urged her.

"I have chosen the book *Wonder* by R. J. Palacio," the queen said with dramatic flair.

"I've been wanting to read that book!" Ellen said.

"Me too," Kirk added.

"What's it about?" Luke asked.

"It's about a boy who has something wrong with his face," Ellen said, proud that she knew.

"The protagonist does indeed have a facial **deformity**," the queen said. "But the book is not about his face. We will discuss what the book is truly about when we have finished reading it," the queen said.

★ ★ ★ ★ ★ ★ ★ ★ ★ ★

deformity – *abnormality*

★ ★ ★ ★ ★ ★ ★ ★ ★ ★

"Let's get started reading it as soon as I have another helping of dessert," the king said. This made everyone laugh.

The royal English family looked forward to reading *Wonder* whenever they did not have evening plans. They read the book quickly because they loved it.

They settled into the library to listen to their mother read the last chapters. The queen's voice was thick with emotion. Ellen dabbed at her eyes. "That was just beautiful," the queen said as she concluded her reading.

"It was," Ellen agreed, sniffling.

"I liked it," Luke said matter-of-factly.

"You liked it? Is that all you have to say?" Ellen chastised him, still sniffling.

"Ellen, I'm a guy," Luke said as if this explained everything.

Ellen rolled her eyes and Kirk laughed.

The king redirected the family's attention. "Now, Ellen, what would you say the book is about?"

Ellen squinted in concentration. "Well, Auggie had something wrong with his face. He went to school and didn't know anyone," Ellen answered.

"Ellen, you're telling me the plot. I want to know the theme of the book," the king said with some impatience.

Ellen shrugged, and the boys mumbled.

"You don't know what the theme is?" the king said wonderingly. His three children sheepishly agreed that they did not. "I'm not going to hide my surprise," the king said, frowning.

He removed *The Guidebook to Grammar Galaxy* from its shelf, paged to the article on theme, and read aloud to them.

Theme
Theme is the meaning or message of a book, poem, or movie.

Some common themes are love conquers all; crime doesn't pay; we are our own worst enemy; we can achieve the impossible with enough effort; money is the root of all evil, and technology will destroy humanity.

Themes are the author's opinion on common subjects such as love, death, human nature, overcoming struggles, growing up, family, good vs. evil, the meaning of life, money, friendship, technology, people vs. nature, people vs. society, and war. There may be multiple themes, but there is usually a primary theme.

To discover the theme of a work, state the plot in one sentence. The plot is not the same as the theme but will give you clues about it. Remember that plot is a problem and a solution. The problem in Cinderella was her mistreatment by her stepfamily. The solution was the prince meeting and choosing her for his bride at the royal ball. So, Cinderella's plot is: A mistreated stepdaughter attends the royal ball and is chosen by the prince as his bride over her mean stepsisters.

Next, note the subject. In addition to the plot, what is the book about? Cinderella is a fairy tale and like many fairy tales is about good vs. evil. A less important subject of Cinderella is love. Many literary works cover more than one subject.

Finally, determine the author's attitude toward the problem and solution. What is the author trying to say? These answers will make the theme clearer. In Cinderella, the author seems to enjoy Cinderella's happiness at the stepfamily's expense. The author seems to be saying that good will eventually win over evil.

If you are correct about the theme, you should be able to find examples to support it. Examples will include characters' actions and quotes. In many versions of Cinderella, the girl is described as "good" and "kind." Her stepsisters are described as "ugly" and "mean." The stepfamily is shocked by the prince's choice of Cinderella as his bride. In some versions, they beg Cinderella for forgiveness. They are either sent away or forgiven, depending on the author's view of what good winning over evil looks like.

"I like it when they're sent away in disgrace," Luke said, chuckling.

"I do too, but your mother doesn't approve," the king agreed, smirking. "Now that we know what theme is, let's talk about the theme of *Wonder*. We've already noted the plot. What subjects is the book about?"

"Having a messed-up face?" Luke asked.

"Not really, Luke. Ellen, what do you think?" the king asked.

"I think it's about friendship," Ellen suggested.

"Yes, but I also think it's about being brave. Overcoming a challenge," Kirk said.

"That's excellent," the king said. "Now what is the author saying about the plot and these subjects?" he asked.

"Hm. Maybe don't give up?" Luke said. "Auggie had a lot of surgeries and a lot of problems with his friends. But he didn't give up and things worked out."

"Luke, good thinking. That is definitely a theme of *Wonder*. Anyone else?" the king asked.

The queen said, "The book says the theme is reading is a waste of time."

Everyone stared at her, mouths **agape**. "What did you say?" the king asked.

"It says the theme is reading is a waste of time. See?" she said, holding up the book. The last page had been stamped with red ink.

★ ★ ★ ★ ★ ★ ★ ★ ★ ★
agape – *open*
desecrated – *damaged*
★ ★ ★ ★ ★ ★ ★ ★ ★ ★

"What on English?" the king exclaimed. "Who would have **desecrated** a book this way?" Before he had finished speaking, the kids were mouthing the name Gremlin. "Screen," the king ordered. "Tell me if there's anything having to do with theme happening on planet Composition."

Screen complied, and the top search result was a story on the opening of a new theme park. The king asked Screen to play the video. A reporter stood in front of a set of gates where books, poems, and scripts were being stamped as they entered. "Zoom in!" the king requested. The royal family was able to see that all these works were being stamped. The stamp read "Theme: Reading is a waste of time."

The reporter noted that only written works were being allowed entry to the theme park. They did not yet have a review of the attractions inside.

Kirk said, "I don't see any attractions from here."

"No," Ellen added. "It looks like an abandoned mall."

"We have to shut it down," the king said urgently. "Themes can be used to change public opinion. If we don't remove the themes from these books, our citizens will start believing that reading is a waste of time! You three children have to go to planet Composition. But first, you'll need to send a mission to the guardians, asking them to identify the real theme of these books. Reading is not a waste of time!"

The three English children agreed and began work on a mission called Theme.

What does *desecrated* mean?

How do you determine a book's theme?

What theme was the theme park stamping on books?

Chapter 2

"What do you think of GASA's plan for dealing with NEOs?" Kirk asked his father at dinner that evening.

"What's GASA stand for again?" Luke asked.

"It's the Galactic Aeronautics and Space Administration," Kirk replied.

"Oh yeah," Luke said nodding. "And what's an NEO?"

"It's a near-English object, better known as an asteroid. It could collide with our planet," Kirk explained.

"Ooh, cool," Luke said, his eyes lighting up.

"NEOs aren't cool, Luke. They could cause massive damage and **casualties**," Kirk **reproved** him.

"But they won't, right? Because GASA has a plan," Luke said to defend himself.

"They do have a plan. They want to—" Kirk started.

★ ★ ★ ★ ★ ★ ★ ★ ★ ★

casualties – *victims*
reproved – *criticized*
condescendingly – *scornfully*

★ ★ ★ ★ ★ ★ ★ ★ ★ ★

"Blow them up?" Luke interjected. "I can help with that!" he said, demonstrating his asteroid blaster technique.

"Actually, no. They're not going to blow them up," Kirk said **condescendingly**. "Their plan is to find the dangerous asteroids before they get close. Then they'll use a kinetic impact approach."

"A kinetic what?" the king asked.

"Impact. They want to send high-speed spacecraft into the path of NEOs to redirect them," Kirk said.

"You mean they really don't want to blow them up?" Luke asked incredulously.

"Correct," Kirk said.

"Kirk, I had not read about this plan and frankly, I find it hard to believe. Where did you read this?" the king asked.

"The latest issue of *Galactic Science*," Kirk answered.

"Do you have it handy so I can read it?" the king asked.

"On my tablet. I'll get it," Kirk said, excusing himself.

When he returned, he handed the tablet to his father. "Here's the article," Kirk said.

The king took it and read aloud. "GASA has outlined its plan for dealing with NEOs or near-English objects. These are commonly known as asteroids. To prevent dangerous collisions of asteroids with our planet, GASA plans to...." The king trailed off.

"What do they plan to do?" the queen asked when the king didn't keep reading.

"There are gray boxes here where the text was. Is this one of those articles where you have to pay to read the whole thing?" the king asked with disgust.

"No, I read the whole article," Kirk said. "You gave me a subscription to *Galactic Science* for my birthday. Let me see it."

The king handed the tablet back to Kirk, and Kirk grew agitated as he scrolled up and down through the article. "I don't understand this," he said. "Let me reboot the tablet."

His family waited patiently for Kirk to load the article again. "There is still content missing!" Kirk said.

"Maybe the plan you read has been changed and they just haven't updated the article," the king suggested. "It wouldn't surprise me if the article you read was in error."

"I don't think it was a mistake, Father," Kirk said in frustration.

"Well, I'll believe that's the plan when I see it," the king said.

Kirk was determined to prove to his father that what he had read was correct. He began researching GASA's NEO plan after dinner. He was pleased when he found a separate article in a different science magazine. But as he read, he found the same information missing. "Do I have to pay to read?" he muttered to himself. He didn't see anything that said the article was for subscribers only. He tried a different article, only to discover that it had missing sentences as well. *Has the plan become secret?* he wondered. *Was his father right that it was inaccurate reporting that was being changed?*

He decided to drop the research for the moment so he could finish his literature homework. His question for *The Bridge to Terabithia* was: "Why does Jess believe he will be the fastest runner in the fifth grade?" Kirk went to skim the first chapter of the book for the answer. He read Jess's prediction that he could be the fastest runner in the fifth grade. His eyes moved down the page. He read about Jess's sister and the cow who watched him run. He noted a paragraph about his school. But then he was startled—not by what he read—but by what he couldn't. There were gray boxes where some paragraphs once were. They were not just any paragraphs but paragraphs that held the information he needed. He had to talk to his father.

When he found him, Kirk explained that the king had been right about the NEO article. But then he noted that all the articles on the subject had missing information. He told his father about the missing paragraphs in *The Bridge to Terabithia* too. "What's going on?" Kirk asked.

The king and Kirk didn't say what they were thinking—that the Gremlin was at it again. They were already trying to find the solution to the problem. "Screen, give us a status report on planet Composition," the king commanded.

"Your Highness, the story most likely to interest you is this one," Screen said, playing a video.

"I'm here on planet Composition where workers on strike," a reporter said. "These sentences and paragraphs say they have been taken advantage of long enough. They refuse to support written work until their wages are increased."

The king was aghast. "Sentences and paragraphs aren't paid. That's ridiculous!"

"So, you don't think they have a valid complaint?" Kirk asked.

"Of course not," the king said with growing irritation. "They have a happy life as part of their contribution to the galaxy."

"But maybe they aren't recognized for their work?" Kirk suggested.

The king sighed and thought for a moment. "It's obvious to me that the Gremlin has convinced these sentences and paragraphs that they need to go on strike. They don't. But they play a very important role in our galaxy. Without them, we can't explain or prove anything. Kirk, call your brother and sister and have them meet us in the library."

Kirk did as he was instructed. When the four family members were in the library, the king explained what was happening. He found the article on supporting evidence in *The Guidebook to Grammar Galaxy*. He asked Ellen to read it aloud.

Supporting Evidence

Supporting evidence is what readers use to form opinions about a written work. It is also what writers use to create believable characters, plots, and arguments.

Supporting evidence includes dialogue, events, and quotes from fictional texts. In nonfiction works, supporting evidence may include statistics, graphs, quotes, and references.

Learning to identify and use supporting evidence improves reading comprehension and writing skills.

"We need to get the supporting evidence back to work or I can't finish my literature homework," Kirk said.

"That's the least of our worries," the king said. "Scientific research will be at a standstill without them."

"What do we do?" Ellen asked.

"You'll need to identify the supporting evidence on planet Composition. Then you'll need to encourage citizens to end this strike," the king said.

"We'll need the guardians' help for sure. There are so many sentences and paragraphs on strike!" Kirk said.

"I think I know how we can get them back to the books and articles that need them," Ellen said.

The three English children began working on a mission called Supporting Evidence.

What does *reproved* mean?

What is supporting evidence?

Why is supporting evidence missing?

Chapter 3

Luke smiled as the librarians tried to contain the children's excitement. He understood their enthusiasm. He was looking forward to seeing David Shannon in person too.

Luke had listened to his mother read the book *No, David!* so many times that he knew it by heart. He would then "read" it to the family. He had become just as obsessed with *Good Boy, Fergus.* Luke was curious what the author and illustrator of such funny books was like in person. He was sure the other kids were too. Many of them held well-loved copies of his books. Perhaps they were hoping Mr. Shannon would autograph them.

Luke checked the time on his communicator. The author was late. Luke hoped he wouldn't be too much longer as the kids were getting louder with impatience. He noticed the head librarian whispering in her assistant's ear. The assistant looked panic-stricken. She motioned for Luke to join them at the front of the room.

"Mr. Shannon isn't coming," she whispered. Luke gasped. "I know," she said. "We're about to tell the children. But we need you to help with the disappointment."

"Me? How?" Luke asked.

"Will you read some of Mr. Shannon's books to the kids? You're a wonderful storyteller and the kids love you."

Luke blushed at the compliment. "I can do that, but I'm no substitute for Mr. Shannon," Luke said.

The librarian assured Luke she only wanted him to read to the kids with his colorful style. She explained to the children that due to unfortunate circumstances, Mr. Shannon wouldn't be joining them. She waited for the kids (and quite a few parents) to express their disappointment. "But we do have a treat for you. Luke English, our resident storyteller, is going to read you a few of Mr. Shannon's books. Who wants to hear *No, David!* first?"

When the kids shouted their approval, Luke began reading. Several **rousing** stories kept the children entertained. And they seemed satisfied as they left the library. Once everyone had gone, Luke asked if the librarians knew why Mr. Shannon hadn't made the appearance.

★ ★ ★ ★ ★ ★ ★ ★ ★ ★

rousing – *exciting*

★ ★ ★ ★ ★ ★ ★ ★ ★ ★

"When he hadn't arrived as planned, I contacted his assistant. The man said that Mr. Shannon wouldn't be writing or making any appearances until further notice. When I asked why, he said he couldn't say, and he ended the call."

"That's weird. I hope he's okay," Luke said. The librarians nodded their agreement.

When Luke arrived home, the king met him to ask what David Shannon was like. "If I hadn't had a meeting, I would have gone with you," the king said.

Luke explained Mr. Shannon's failure to appear and the mysterious call to his assistant.

"Hm. Must be a personal matter. I'm proud of you for stepping in as a reader, Luke. I'm sure it helped the kids get past their disappointment." The king put his arm around his son and Luke glowed with pride.

The next morning, the king frowned while reading the paper. "What is it, dear?" the queen asked.

"This article says several authors have recently announced their retirement," the king explained.

"Retirement from writing? I didn't think authors retired. You can write your whole life, can't you? I plan to," the queen said.

"Yes. What's stranger is that the authors seem to have disappeared. They can't be reached for comment." The queen agreed this was very odd. "I wonder if David Shannon's failure to appear at the library yesterday is related," the king said. "I'm contacting the GBI. Something is wrong, and I want to get to the bottom of it before more authors disappear."

Soon the king was speaking on screen with the director of the Galactic Bureau of Intelligence. "I read the article about author disappearances in the *Grammar Gazette* this morning. I'm worried. I want you to make finding them a top priority," the king said.

"I'm afraid I can't do that," the director said.

The king was astonished. "Why not?" he asked.

"Because these authors are a part of the Author Protection Program. I can't help you find them because they're in danger."

"From what?"

"Numerous authors have received letters threatening them if they continue writing. We consider it a **credible** threat. We are in the process of trying to find the **perpetrator**."

★ ★ ★ ★ ★ ★ ★ ★ ★ ★
credible – *believable*
perpetrator – *wrongdoer*
★ ★ ★ ★ ★ ★ ★ ★ ★ ★

"The authors received the same letter? May I see it?" the king asked.

The director retrieved a copy from his desk and showed it to the king.

"Our top theory is that a jealous author is sending the letters," the director said.

"I couldn't disagree more," the king said, shaking his head. "It's obvious to me that the Gremlin is sending these letters. The Gremlin is a threat to the English language, but he has no history of violence. There's no reason for writers to stop writing."

"Your Majesty, we have to take the threat seriously. We don't know for certain that the Gremlin sent the letters. It's better to be sure the authors are safe."

"I'd like to talk with the authors about my theory and they can decide whether to take the risk to keep writing. I need to know where to find them."

"I'm sorry, Your Majesty, but we can't give out that information—even to you. We don't know who we can trust."

"That's preposterous!" the king roared before regaining control. "I'm the king of this galaxy. My top concern is protecting the English language, our books, and our citizens. I need to talk with these authors."

"I'm sorry, Your Highness. I'm duty bound to hide their locations until we find whoever is threatening them."

The king sighed and ended the call respectfully.

The queen had listened to the call and watched her husband as he paced. "What are you going to do?" she asked.

"I'm going to get the guardians to help," he replied.

"The kids? But what if this really is a crazy person threatening authors? It could be dangerous," the queen warned.

"What I need them to do isn't dangerous. I promise," the king reassured her.

When Kirk, Luke, and Ellen joined their parents in the dining room, the king explained his conversation with the GBI director. He shared his plan for using the guardians to help him locate the authors.

"Cool! We're going to be like private detectives!" Luke exclaimed. "But how?" he asked.

The king called for *The Guidebook to Grammar Galaxy*. When it was brought to him, he opened the book to the article called "Author Study." He instructed Luke to read it.

Author Study

An author study is an investigation of an author's work and life. The study includes reading multiple books by an author to determine writing style, character types, and common themes. Biographical information and interviews connect the author's personal life to written work. Finally, an author study is an opportunity to compare and contrast personal experiences with an author's or with his or her characters'.

Author studies improve reading and critical thinking skills. They also expose readers to a variety of genres and writing styles. Author studies develop a fondness for books, authors, and fellow readers.

"Doing an author study sounds like fun," Ellen said. "But how will it help us find the missing authors?" she asked.

"I think I know," Kirk said. "By reading multiple books by the same author and learning about them personally, we should gain some clues about where they could be hiding. We may be able to find them and convince them that they aren't in danger. Maybe we can also tell them how much their books mean to us, so they will realize they have to keep writing."

"I couldn't have said it better myself!" the king exclaimed. "I should be able to get the Grammar Patrol to help us once we have a general location to explore," he added.

"We need to send this mission out right away," Luke said. "The Gremlin is probably sending new letters every day."

The family agreed and the three English children began work on a mission called Author Study.

What does *credible* mean?

What's one benefit of doing an author study?

Why are authors missing?

Chapter 4

"Finish your breakfast, children, because I want to leave soon," the queen said.

"Where are you going?" Luke asked, slurping milk from his spoon.

"It's where are *we* going, and don't slurp," she chastised Luke.

"Okay. Where are *we* going?" he asked.

"*We* are going on a nature walk," the queen announced **ceremoniously**.

"A nature walk? You mean a hike?" Ellen asked.

"Yes. It's a hike we take specifically to learn about nature," the queen answered.

★ ★ ★ ★ ★ ★ ★ ★ ★ ★

ceremoniously – *grandly*
implored – *pleaded*

★ ★ ★ ★ ★ ★ ★ ★ ★ ★

"Does that mean it's a hike that's work?" Luke asked, smirking at his siblings.

"If you believe that learning is work, then yes. I happen to believe learning is play. I love learning!" the queen said. She was brimming with enthusiasm for the day she had planned.

Luke didn't seem convinced the nature walk would be fun.

"I wish I could go with you," the king said, sighing. "I have an important meeting today."

"You can't reschedule?" the queen **implored**.

"I'm afraid not. You four have fun, and I'll go along next time," he said firmly.

Luke suddenly brightened. "Can we—I mean, may we bring Comet?"

"Luke, normally I would say yes, but I'm afraid he would scare away any wildlife on the trail," the queen said.

Luke knew better than to argue with her.

The queen gave the children orders to pack water, a notebook, and some colored pencils.

"I knew it was going to be work," Luke grumbled to himself. He felt better about the walk when he saw Cook handing his mother some snacks to take with them.

Later that morning, the English family (minus the king) started down a trail that was new to them. Luke was the first to express his enthusiasm for it.

"This is a cool trail!" he exclaimed. He hoped to make up for his earlier **reticence**.

★ ★ ★ ★ ★ ★ ★ ★ ★ ★
reticence – *reluctance*
★ ★ ★ ★ ★ ★ ★ ★ ★ ★

"I knew you would like it," the queen said, grinning.

"What kind of nature study will we be doing, Mother?" Kirk asked.

"All sorts of things," the queen answered. "But let's get started by looking for adjectives."

"Adjectives on a hike? They're in Adjective Alley on planet Sentence, aren't they?" Kirk asked.

"That's where the words live, yes. But we see adjectives all around us. Green is an adjective. Find something green," the queen said.

"Oh, that's easy." Ellen said. "This leaf is green." She picked it up and handed it to her mother.

"What tree did this leaf come from?" her mother asked.

"That one," Ellen said, pointing overhead.

"Right, but what type of tree is it?" the queen asked. When Ellen said she didn't know, the queen handed her a tree identification guide. "See if you can find this type of leaf in here," she said.

"I'll help you find it," Luke volunteered.

Kirk held his communicator above another similar leaf and waited for confirmation. Then he proclaimed, "It's from an oak tree."

"No fair, Kirk!" his siblings objected.

"Kirk, let's use nature guides on this hike, okay?" the queen suggested, putting her arm around her oldest son. "But you are correct. These are oak leaves. Get out your notebooks and draw them and label them oak leaves. Then you'll remember what kind of leaf they are next time."

"Aw, I can't draw, Mother," Luke objected.

"I think you mean that drawing takes you longer than you like because you haven't practiced," the queen corrected him.

"Okay, that, but either way I don't like to draw," Luke said.

24

"Why don't you trace the leaf? Tracing will be faster," the queen said.

Luke agreed and started tracing an oak leaf on a notebook page. The queen encouraged the three of them to add the leaf's veins and color the drawing to match the leaf as they saw it.

"When you're finished, be sure to date the page. These leaves will be changing color soon. It would be nice to have a drawing of them in the fall too," she said.

"The new life will be fading into old age and then death," Luke said.

"Uh, that's a dramatic way of putting it, but yes," the queen said.

A rustling in the bushes near them got their attention. "A fox!" Ellen exclaimed, pointing as the animal darted away from them.

When they could see it no longer, the queen suggested they learn more about foxes. "I don't have a guide on forest animals with me. I'll have to ask you to use your communicator, Kirk," the queen said sheepishly.

"They're sly and clever," Luke said. "He was listening to our conversation. Probably a Gremlin scout," Luke said.

The queen laughed. "Luke, that's not exactly a scientific description of a fox." Before she could ask Kirk what he'd found about foxes, she felt drops of rain on her head and forearms. "Rain?" she said with annoyance. "The forecast said nothing about rain today."

"Sadness, despair," Ellen said.

"Oh, it's not that serious," the queen said. "We can use the rain. We'll just have to cut our nature walk short and come back another day."

Up ahead on the trail, the queen spotted someone walking quickly toward them. As she moved closer, the queen saw that it was a woman wearing a cloak. She was pulling the hood down over her face as she approached. "Looks like we're going to get rained on," the queen said to her.

The woman said nothing as she swished past them.

"Human trickery," Ellen said.

"What did you say?" the queen asked, frowning. "She's just trying to get out of the rain."

The rain began to fall more steadily. The queen urged the children to pack their notebooks and follow her out of the woods. Lightning lit up the sky behind them.

"Power, strength," Kirk said.

"It is powerful and it's dangerous for us to be out in this storm. Hurry!" the queen said.

After the family boarded the space tram for the trip home, the queen tried to make the best of the weather. "We can learn more about what causes rain and how it affects the plants in the forest," she said.

"Look!" Ellen exclaimed, pointing out the window. "A big black bird. What kind is it?"

"It's a raven," Kirk said. "Death, destruction, impending doom."

"What are you talking about, Kirk? It's just a raven. A big black bird. Nothing more. You children are giving me the creeps today. I'm looking forward to the sun returning," the queen said, staring out the window.

Thunder rumbled and shook the windows of the tram. "Wrath, punishment," Ellen said.

"Seriously, stop," the queen said, shivering. "It's just thunder!"

The group was silent during the trip home, but the queen was worried. *What had gotten into her children to make them so negative?* she wondered.

Cook met them at the door as they returned to the castle. "So sorry your nature walk was rained out," she said. "Would you like an apple as a snack? These are fresh from the local orchard."

"Temptation, loss of innocence," Luke said.

Cook looked to the queen with raised eyebrows. The queen began to answer her unspoken question. "Ever since we were in the forest—"

"A place of evil or mystery," Kirk interjected.

"That's been happening," the queen said, gesturing toward Kirk.

"Oh my word," Cook said, wide-eyed. "How about some cookies then?"

The children nodded silently and munched on some cookies and milk.

The queen used the opportunity to find her husband. She had to tell him how strangely the children were behaving.

She found him in his office, holding a large sword. "What is that?" she shrieked, stepping backward.

"Protection and strength," the king answered.

"Not you too," the queen said, collapsing into a chair.

"I know why you're here," the king said.

"If you say something creepy, I'm leaving," the queen threatened.

The king laughed and put the sword away. "I'll try not to. I have been made aware of a situation in Symbolism City. Every word that has been a symbol in literature has been given orders to move to Symbolism City. Supposedly, by my order. But I think we both know who is behind it."

The queen nodded. "What are you going to do?"

"I'm going to have the children direct the efforts to return the words home. But first, they need to know what symbolism is."

The queen nodded again, then shrieked, as she saw the eyes of the king's owl statue blink. "It—it—blinked!" she stammered, pointing at the owl.

"Ah yes, wisdom," he said calmly.

"I'm going to my bedchamber until you get these symbols under control!" the queen said, exiting briskly.

The king used his communicator to have the children and *The Guidebook to Grammar Galaxy* brought to him. Then he read the entry on symbolism to them.

Symbolism

A symbol is a setting, character, event, or object in a story that has a deeper meaning. Symbols are literal (observable) and figurative (metaphorical).

The ring in *The Lord of the Rings* symbolizes power and evil.

The lion in *The Lion, The Witch, and the Wardrobe* symbolizes power and authority.

The garden in *The Secret Garden* symbolizes a safe place.

An entire plot can be symbolic. Symbolic plots are called **allegories**. The plot of the movie *Wall-E* symbolizes saving the earth. The book *The Sneetches* by Dr. Seuss symbolizes racism.

Authors can create new symbolism in their work or rely on accepted meanings. Some commonly understood symbols are listed in the chart below.

Note that too many symbols in a literary work can make it silly.

Symbolism Chart	
SETTINGS	
Forest: often evil, the unknown	**Rainbow:** good fortune
Desert: loneliness	**Rain:** sadness
Garden: paradise or safe place	**Storms:** strong emotions
Spring: fresh start	**Lightning:** power
Winter: death	**Apple:** temptation
Dawn, light, candle: hope	**Weeds:** evil
Darkness, night: danger	**Rose:** romance
Fog: confusion	**Water:** purity
Thunder, fire: punishment	**Evergreen tree:** eternal life
COLORS	
Black: death, evil	**Blue:** peace
White: good	**Yellow:** aging
Red: emotion	**Gold:** wealth
Green: life	**Purple:** royalty
OBJECTS	
Cloak: trickery	**Circle:** perfection
Mask: demonic	**Pearl:** purity
Skull: death	**Ring:** commitment
Crown: power	**Sword:** protection
Key: answer	**Axe:** work
Heart: love	
ANIMALS	
Dove: peace	**Fox, cat:** clever
Eagle: freedom	**Peacock:** pride
Lion, bear: power	**Raven:** death
Dog: loyalty	**Owl:** wisdom
Butterfly: change	**Lamb:** gentleness

When his father finished reading, Luke removed a decorative axe from his father's wall. He announced, "We better get to work."

"Luke, put that back. But you're right. The excess symbolism is upsetting your mother. I need you three to send the symbols who were recently invited to Symbolism City home. You'll need the guardians' help of course."

The children nodded. "Look! A rainbow!" Ellen exclaimed, pointing out the window.

Kirk started to speak but was interrupted by his father. "Don't say it. Just get to work on the mission." The kids laughed and created a mission called Symbolism for the guardians.

What does *implored* mean?

What do rainbows symbolize?

Why were the English children stating symbolic meanings on their nature walk?

Chapter 5

It was family movie night and the royal English family was seated in the media room with plenty of popcorn. They were watching *The Wizard of Oz*. The family had read the book and was looking forward to watching the film version.

When one of the farmhands accused Dorothy of not having any brains, a shadow passed across the screen.

"That was weird," Kirk said.

Ellen cringed when Ms. Gulch demanded that Dorothy hand over Toto. Another shadow passed over the screen. When the family looked to the king, he said, "It's an old movie." Everyone nodded.

When Dorothy went to visit Professor Marvel, a shadow passed over the screen again. "It keeps happening," Luke complained.

"Yes, it does. At certain points in the film, a shadow appears," Kirk said. The family was startled when some **sinister** music—duhn, duhn, duhn—played behind them.

★ ★ ★ ★ ★ ★ ★ ★ ★ ★
sinister – *creepy*
ominous – *threatening*
★ ★ ★ ★ ★ ★ ★ ★ ★ ★

"Was that music from the movie?" the queen asked.

"That was amazing surround-sound audio," Kirk said. "Did you just have that installed?" he asked the king.

"Yes! It's marvelous, isn't it?" the king said, congratulating himself. "Let's keep watching the movie. Maybe the rest of the film will be okay."

The family continued watching and didn't notice more shadows. The king asked them questions about the differences between the book and the movie.

When they were through talking, Luke said, "I'm glad I don't have any work to do tomorrow. And no tornadoes in the forecast," he said joking. The **ominous** music played again.

"I thought I asked Screen to turn off those speakers," the king said.

"They are powered off, Your Majesty," Screen said.

"Perhaps it was a power surge," Kirk suggested. The king agreed that explained the speakers being on briefly. He announced that it was late and said everyone should say good night.

Luke decided to start a new book before bed. He was near the end of the first chapter when a shadow moved across the pages. He looked around wildly, thinking something was flying in his bedchamber. Was it a large moth? A bird? A bat? He scanned every corner of the room but saw nothing. He turned off the light and tried to sleep but couldn't. He decided to tell his father what he had seen, just in case.

The king wasn't too happy to find Luke knocking at his bedchamber door. He yawned loudly. "Luke, it was probably your own hand casting a shadow on your book," he said after Luke explained what he'd seen.

Luke considered this. "Yes, it could have been," he said, feeling relieved.

After Luke returned to his room, the king told his wife, "I think *The Wizard of Oz* was too scary for Luke. He's seeing things."

"That makes sense," the queen murmured as she read a book of her own.

31

The king rolled over to try to sleep. He was nearly snoozing when the queen screamed. The king bolted upright. "What is it?" he cried.

"It…there was a shadow on my book. I think there's something in the room. Maybe a bat. Catch it, dear!" the queen shrieked, jumping out of bed.

The king turned on all the lights and searched the room for any type of flying creature. When he found none, he gave his wife the same explanation he'd given Luke. "I think *The Wizard of Oz* was too much for you too!" he said, laughing. "Go to sleep, dear."

The king was lying peacefully with his eyes closed and was nearly asleep when he sat upright again. "The Foreshadow," he whispered. "He's here!"

The king got out of bed, trying not to disturb the queen. He put on his robe and slippers and walked to his office. When there, he asked Screen to check social media for reports of unusual shadows and sounds. He wasn't surprised to read reports of shadows in books, movies, and even plays. The Foreshadow was on planet English where he was frightening people. No doubt the Gremlin had helped him in his **quest** to leave planet Composition.

★ ★ ★ ★ ★ ★ ★ ★ ★ ★

quest – *mission*

★ ★ ★ ★ ★ ★ ★ ★ ★ ★

He considered waking the children but decided against it. They could help him in the morning.

At breakfast, the king explained his theory about the Foreshadow. He already had *The Guidebook to Grammar Galaxy* at the table. He asked Luke to read the entry on foreshadowing.

Foreshadowing
Foreshadowing is a literary technique in which clues about future events are given at the beginning of a story. Foreshadowing builds suspense and interest in the plot. It keeps readers reading and viewers watching. Some movie genres use music to draw attention to foreshadowing.   An example of foreshadowing in the Disney film *Bambi* is Bambi's mother warning him of the danger of Man with a gun. This is a clue to his mother being killed by a hunter later in the film.

"Oh, I remember that. It was soooo sad," Ellen said. "Foreshadow is a bad guy, making us sad like that. We have to send him back to planet Composition right away."

"Not all foreshadowing is sad, Ellen," the king corrected her. "For example, foreshadowing in love stories hints that a couple will be together in the end."

"Aww," Ellen said. "I love that kind of foreshadowing."

"I like guessing the end of the story because of foreshadowing," Kirk said. "Sending him back won't remove foreshadowing, right, Father?"

"No, not at all. A little foreshadowing in literature is a good thing," the king said.

"I just want to know how we can get that dreadful Foreshadow off our planet," the queen said nervously.

"Dear, the guardians are going to take care of it. Don't worry," the king said.

"How are we going to get him back to planet Composition?" Luke asked.

"You'll look for examples of foreshadowing to help us locate him. Then we need a way to entice him home," the king said.

"I have an idea," Luke said smiling.

The three English children set to work preparing a mission called Foreshadowing.

What does *quest* mean?

How is music a part of foreshadowing?

Why are people seeing a shadow on planet English?

Chapter 6

"Ah, that's right. It's Galactic History Month," the king said, reading the paper aloud to the queen.

"Oh, lovely. I do so enjoy the documentaries they show on the Galactic History Channel this time of year," the queen said. "Are there any other special activities planned?" she asked.

"Let's see," the king said, scanning the paper. "There is a special display at the art museum of previous kings' and queens' artifacts," he said.

"I must go to see the dresses," the queen gushed. "They're my favorite."

"The History Museum is planning a special emphasis on literary history this month. They'll have a display of our oldest books."

"I'll have to take the children to see them," the queen said. "I was looking at a very old book in a glass case that opened. It wasn't locked. When I lifted the lid to touch it, an alarm sounded. I was **rebuked** by the museum **personnel**. I was so embarrassed," the queen said, covering her face.

★ ★ ★ ★ ★ ★ ★ ★ ★ ★
rebuked – *scolded*
personnel – *workers*
★ ★ ★ ★ ★ ★ ★ ★ ★ ★

"When did this happen?" the king asked, obviously agitated by his wife's story.

The queen's focus returned to her husband. She seemed surprised by the question. "Oh. I don't know. I was maybe five or six?" she said.

"Good grammar! I thought this had just happened," the king said in an irritated tone.

"Oh, no. Sorry. I was just remembering," the queen apologized.

"Well, remind the children not to touch any of the rare books," the king said. The queen agreed.

At breakfast that morning, the royal family discussed history month. The king asked the children for their favorite periods of history. "I love the medieval period," Luke said. "I had on my armor and my trusty sword and I slew the mightiest dragon in the village." Luke demonstrated his swordsmanship.

The rest of the family chuckled but frowned in concern when Luke continued. "I drove my sword right into the heart of the beast. I drug it to the castle and presented it to the king."

"Luke, is this one of the stories you tell the kids at the library?" Ellen asked.

Luke seemed disoriented. "Stories?" he asked.

"Yes, you started telling us about how you were a knight killing a dragon," Ellen said. The rest of the family nodded.

"Oh. Oh, yes. That's what I loved to do when I was little. Remember, Kirk? I would make a dragon out of pillows and the castle was made of giant Legos," Luke explained.

"I'd forgotten all about that," Kirk said, smiling. "You would have me be the king who congratulated you."

"That's right! And I would be the **damsel** in distress," Ellen said, remembering. "That was so much fun."

★ ★ ★ ★ ★ ★ ★ ★ ★ ★

damsel – *lady*

★ ★ ★ ★ ★ ★ ★ ★ ★ ★

Cook emerged from the kitchen to ask how the family liked the new pastry she'd prepared. When everyone agreed it was delicious, she said, "I burned my hand." The family exclaimed their sympathies as she continued. "I had wanted to bake, but Mother said I was too young to help. So when she left the kitchen, I reached into the oven. I wanted to see if the pastries were getting brown. I pulled the pan toward me and blistered my fingers. I didn't want her to know I'd disobeyed her, so I nursed them myself. I never cried."

The English family seemed confused. "I thought you had just now burned your hand!" the queen said.

"Me too," Luke agreed.

"You never told me that story," the queen said, her eyes welling with tears.

Cook cradled her fingers, remembering the pain. Then she noticed that she was the center of the family's attention. "For galaxy's sake, I'm forgetting myself!" she apologized. "I'm heading back to the kitchen." The family assured her she had done nothing wrong before she left.

"That was a little weird," Luke said. His mother hushed him.

"It's not good manners to say it, but I agree with Luke. People are speaking strangely today. My father had a model spaceship that he had spent hours working on. I was forbidden to touch it. But one day, I looked for him in his office and he wasn't there. I came close to the spaceship. I touched the windows ever so gently. But the model was old, and that little bit of pressure moved a window pane. When I tried to replace it, another window pane came loose. I was frantic. I asked our butler to help me find some adhesive so I could put it back together. We fixed it and he never told my father. I've always loved him for that."

"Dear, you've never told me that story. But why are you telling us now? You said people were talking strangely. Then you started talking as though you were a young boy," the queen said.

The king seemed lost in thought but suddenly became alert. "Why did I start talking about that? I was just noticing how you and Luke and Cook were...my word! We are flashing back!" he exclaimed.

"Flashing back?" Kirk asked. "What do you mean?"

"I need *The Guidebook to Grammar Galaxy*. Kirk, will you get it for me?" the king asked.

Kirk left to retrieve the book and when he returned, he read the article on flashback as requested by his father.

Flashback
A flashback in a book or movie is an interruption of the present time with a scene from the past. Flashbacks can help explain events and characters' behavior.

Flashbacks in literature should not be overused. They do provide information. But they stop the action that keeps readers and viewers engaged. Use flashbacks sparingly, keep them short, and don't use them near the beginning of a story.

Flashbacks may be identified using the following as clues: a line break in the text, references to the past (e.g., an hour earlier), or use of the past perfect tense (e.g., She had struggled with spelling.)

Clues that the book has returned to the present include references to circumstances before the flashback (e.g., The pain in her leg disturbed her thoughts.) or use of simple past tense (e.g., She ate her eggs and asked for help adjusting her pillow).

"I was reading a book when the whole setting changed," Luke said.

"Luke, are you having a flashback?" Ellen asked.

"No! I was just saying that flashbacks can be confusing," Luke said defensively.

"They can be, Luke. That's why I'm worried. I don't know what the Gremlin's done that is causing all the flashbacks," the king said.

"Do you think it could have anything to do with History Month?" the queen asked.

"Hm. Flashbacks do provide information from the past. But they're not exactly history," the king said.

"What if the Gremlin used History Month as an excuse to add flashback to written works?" Kirk suggested.

"There's one way to find out," the king said. "Screen, connect me with the head librarian of the Galactic Historical Society."

When the librarian appeared on the screen, the king greeted him warmly. "I wondered if you are aware of any new programs involving history and literature?" he asked.

"Why, yes! The Historical Society believes it is important that history is kept. Historical writing is being featured on planet Composition this month," he said.

"What do you mean by *featured*?" the king asked.

"We left the details to staff on planet Composition," the librarian answered.

"Uh-oh," Luke said before being hushed.

When the king ended the call, he shared his suspicion with his family. "I'm afraid the planet is overcrowded with historical paragraphs. They are likely being added to books and movies where they don't belong. There are so many of them that they're even coming up in our conversations."

"Wow. I was walking in the garden alone one morning and..." Ellen began.

"Ellen, we don't have time for another flashback," Kirk said. "We need to go to planet Composition and put the historical paragraphs back where they belong."

Ellen realized what she had been doing and agreed. The three of them worked together to create a mission called Flashback. They knew they would need the guardians' help.

What does *personnel* mean?

What can a flashback help explain?

Why is everyone having flashbacks?

Chapter 7

"Luke, this morning, you're going to get this room cleaned and organized," the queen said firmly. She **surveyed** his bedchamber with disdain.

"I will," Luke said grudgingly.

"See that you do. There will be no games of any sort until it's done," the queen said before leaving him.

Luke sighed. It would take him forever to clean his room. But he knew his mother wouldn't budge on her gaming rule. He picked up the book on his bed, intending to put it away. Then he remembered that he didn't know whether the hero had escaped the trap the **villain**

★ ★ ★ ★ ★ ★ ★ ★ ★ ★
surveyed – *examined*
villain – *antihero*
★ ★ ★ ★ ★ ★ ★ ★ ★ ★

had set for him. It would take him no time to see what happened. And besides, reading was more important than a clean room!

Luke quickly read a chapter of the book only to discover he still didn't know if the hero would escape. He would have to read one more chapter to find out what happened. After that chapter, Luke realized he didn't have much more of the book left. He may as well read the whole thing. Then he could focus on cleaning his room.

Luke wasn't sure how much time had passed when his mother reappeared at his door. "Luke!" she shrieked. "You haven't done a thing in here!"

Luke was startled and then ashamed. "I'm sorry, Mother. I was just going to read a chapter of this book because it's so good. And then I forgot about my room," he said apologetically.

"All right. Give me the book. I'm going to stay here and supervise. Make your bed," the queen ordered. As she continued to direct Luke's cleaning efforts, her brow furrowed in worry. *What was wrong with Luke?* she wondered.

That evening, the queen shared her concern with her husband. "I think something may be wrong with our son."

"Because he doesn't want to clean his room? If that's a disorder, it's an epidemic," the king said, chuckling.

"I'm serious, dear. The boy can't seem to focus. It isn't just his room. He is easily distracted when he is studying too," the queen explained.

The king sighed. "I'm not worried about it. But I can see that you are. Make an appointment to have him checked out," he said, hoping to appease her. The queen smiled and hugged her husband.

The queen arranged an appointment with Dr. **Accomplice.** He was a doctor who specialized in behavior problems. The doctor later met with both of them and asked many questions. He asked the queen to come back alone to get Luke's diagnosis the next day.

★ ★ ★ ★ ★ ★ ★ ★ ★ ★

accomplice – *partner in crime*

★ ★ ★ ★ ★ ★ ★ ★ ★ ★

"I'm afraid the results are what I expected," the doctor told the queen in his office.

"What is it?" the queen asked frightfully.

"It's hyperbole. Luke's mind is highly active. That is not unusual in genius students like your son," he explained.

"Luke's a genius?" the queen asked incredulously.

"Yes. In fact, I would say he is one of the greatest minds of our time. It's quite a privilege you have of raising him."

The queen struggled to believe what she was hearing and then came to acceptance. She said, "All right. We will have to help him use his gift. But what about his trouble focusing?" she asked.

"Luke is so intelligent and quick that it's best you do not push him to do anything that will slow him down. Reading and chores, in particular, should be avoided."

The queen studied the doctor's license on the wall. "Are you sure I shouldn't encourage him to read and do chores?" she asked.

"Under no circumstances should he be encouraged to read. And messiness is part of being a genius," the doctor stated confidently.

The queen thanked him for his help and left. On the way home, she kept shaking her head. She wondered if she had heard the doctor correctly. *Luke was a genius? One of the greatest minds on the planet? And she wasn't to encourage him to read or do chores like cleaning his room?* She couldn't wait to talk with the king about it.

When the queen told her husband what the doctor had said, his reaction surprised her. "That's the best news I've ever heard!" he exclaimed.

"It is? Don't you think it's a bit odd?" the queen asked.

"No, that Doctor Accomplice is our top education expert. We should trust what he says," the king said.

"He's the top education expert? How do you know that?" the queen asked.

"Because we live in the greatest galaxy in the universe. He attended the finest university in the galaxy. He's written for the best journals we have, so he is our top expert," the king said.

"I didn't know you'd looked into him," the queen said, still not trusting her husband.

Ellen burst into the king's study and interrupted their conversation. "The castle is freezing!" she complained. "I feel like I'm in the arctic with no coat on. We have to do something or I'm going to die!" she said, shivering.

"It's a little cool in here, but I wouldn't say it's freezing," the queen said. "Are you ill?" she asked, feeling Ellen's forehead.

Just then, Kirk interrupted them. "It's happened. There's a computer virus that is so powerful that it will shut down every system in the galaxy. It's the end of the world," he said, obviously terrified.

"What on English is going on?" the queen asked. She looked to her husband for guidance, but he seemed distracted.

"I'm the smartest king this galaxy has ever had," the king bragged. "I can solve this computer virus problem with a snap of my fingers."

The queen knew then that whatever was wrong was affecting her husband too. Ever since she had heard Luke's diagnosis, something was bothering her. Hyperbole. She'd heard of it before.

She headed to the library and asked Screen to give her search results on hyperbole. The first article said it was a disorder with symptoms of constant movement, acting without thinking, a short attention span, and being easily distracted.

Some of that sounds like Luke, she thought. At the end of the article, a sentence caught her eye: "Also known as Attention Deficit Hyperactivity Disorder or ADHD."

"Yes! I've heard of ADHD," the queen said. "So, it's called hyperbole now? That doesn't seem right." She thought for a moment and pulled *The Guidebook to Grammar Galaxy* from the shelf. She was elated when she found an article on hyperbole in the table of contents. She read the article quickly.

Hyperbole

Hyperbole is an exaggeration or overstatement. It is used to create an emotional response in readers and listeners. *Hyper* means over, beyond, or excessive. Statements of hyperbole are not meant to be taken literally. Some examples include:

This backpack weighs a ton.
I've told you to clean your room a million times.
He was the greatest salesman who ever lived.

A little hyperbole can help readers and listeners form pictures in their minds. It can encourage them to take action. Hyperbole is used for good effect in literature, songs, speeches, and advertisements. However, hyperbole would not be appropriate in some nonfiction works like science journals.

After reading, the queen began thinking aloud. "Hyperbole is not the same thing as ADHD. Why are they listed as the same thing online? And why is everyone in this house using hyperbole?" She thought a moment. "Screen, give me a status update on planet Sentence," she commanded.

"Your Highness, here is a list of the top news stories from the planet," Screen responded.

The queen looked them over and then tapped to open the story with this headline: "Hyperbole Program Designed to Make Grammar Galaxy the Best, Strongest, and Fastest in the universe."

The article quoted Dr. Accomplice. "For years, we've treated people with Attention Deficit Hyperactivity Disorder (that I've renamed hyperbole) like there's something wrong with them. The fact is that they think and act faster than the rest of us. That's a good thing! They should be allowed to use their superior gifts as they choose. They shouldn't be asked to read, which takes too long. They shouldn't have to waste time trying to be neat when messiness is part of their genius."

"That's what he told me," the queen said to herself. She continued reading. The article said that Dr. Accomplice was working with planet leaders to encourage hyperbole, not discourage it. As a result, sentences that had been labeled hyperbole were being sent to planet Composition ahead of others.

"We believe that encouraging hyperbole will make us the greatest galaxy in the universe," Dr. Accomplice had said.

"This is the worst thing that could ever happen!" the queen said out loud. Then she gasped. "I just used hyperbole. I've got to tell my family what's going on," she said, rushing back to the king's study with the guidebook.

She was glad to find Luke had joined the rest of the family there. She explained what she had learned about the hyperbole program and Dr. Accomplice's recommendations. Then she read the guidebook article to them.

"That was the greatest article in the guidebook we've read so far," Luke said.

The queen sighed. "That's more hyperbole, Luke."

"Dr. Accomplice is obviously working with the Gremlin to get kids to stop reading," the king said.

"And to stop doing chores," the queen added.

"Is that part really that bad?" Luke joked.

43

"You three children will have to go to planet Composition and find every single bit of hyperbole," the king said.

"Every bit?" Ellen said, imagining how much work it would be.

The king realized he had used hyperbole and changed his mind. "You'll need the guardians' help to find *some* hyperbole and send it back to planet Sentence. While you're gone, I will work with planet authorities to shut down the hyperbole program," he said.

"First, can we raise the temperature in here, so I don't freeze to death?" Ellen said.

"And can I first work with our programmer on the virus that's going to be the end of the world?" Kirk asked.

"And can Luke first clean his room that looks like a tornado hit it?" the queen asked.

"I believe that if we work on the hyperbole problem first, none of these other problems will seem as bad. That's what I think, anyway, as the greatest king this galaxy has ever had," the king said.

The kids looked at one another knowingly and said, "We better get going to planet Composition."

"And we'll need to send out a mission," Luke added.

"That reminds me. I need to find some tips on Attention Deficit Hyperactivity Disorder. Then you can include them in your mission," the queen said. "I'm sure you're not the only genius guardian who is easily distracted, Luke."

"Genius?" all three kids asked.

"Let's discuss this when we don't have a hyperbole problem," the queen joked. The kids laughed and got to work on a mission called Hyperbole.

What does *surveyed* mean?

What can hyperbole help readers and listeners do?

Why is the English family using too much hyperbole?

44

Chapter 8

The royal family had just sat down to watch their favorite comedy show when the king was **summoned** by the butler.

"Your Highness," the butler said in the hallway outside the media room. "The Prime Minister is waiting for you on a conference call in your office."

The king raised his eyebrows, surprised to be getting a call so late in the evening. He made his way to the office hastily, assuming the matter was urgent.

"Mr. Prime Minister," the king said when he arrived. "To what do I owe the honor?"

"I'm so sorry to bother you at this late hour, Your Majesty. I just thought you should know that the humor writers have gone on strike."

"A writers' strike? There's no doubt they deserve more money. But it will eventually affect our television programming if it's not **resolved**."

"Yes. And there's more. Out of sympathy for the humor writers, book stores have agreed to stop selling humorous books."

The king gasped. "That's an extreme step! At least we have the library to get us by until the strike has ended."

"I'm afraid not, Sire. The president of the Galactic Library Association has agreed to make all humorous materials unavailable for checkout. That means books and movies too."

"You can't be serious!" the king exclaimed.

"I'm afraid I am," the Prime Minister said soberly.

"Well then. I suppose this is effective immediately?"

"It is."

"I'll have to break the news to my family that we won't be watching our favorite show tonight," the king said.

"I'm sorry, Your Majesty. Let me know if there is anything I can do to help."

"I will," the king said before ending the call.

Before the king could give his family the news, Luke announced that the king hadn't missed anything. "There's no new episode on!" he said, disappointed. "We're watching the *Galaxy's Funniest Home Videos* instead."

"You are?" the king asked.

"Why do you seem surprised, dear?" the queen asked.

"Because I just learned that there is a humor writers' strike. Humorous books aren't being sold or made available to check out from the library. Funny TV shows and movies aren't going to be available either. They won't be until the writers and publishers come to an agreement."

"I guess this show is on because it's regular people's videos?" Luke suggested.

"I guess so," the king said, smiling. "At least we have something funny to watch, right?" His family agreed and paid attention to the screen.

A baseball player was ready to catch the ball when he was hit in the head. The host said, "I wondered why the ball was getting bigger. Then it hit me." The king groaned.

A little girl was carrying an ice cream cone when she tripped. It flew into the air and was snatched by a Dalmatian. "That hit the spot," the host said.

"Oh, I get it," Ellen said. "The Dalmatian has spots," she giggled.

"I thought the humor writers were on strike," the queen said.

"They are. Maybe the people who write puns aren't though. It's the lowest form of humor," the king said scornfully.

"What's a pun?" Luke asked.

"That's an excellent question," the king said. "In fact, I think we should learn more about humor while we wait for this strike to end. When the show's over, let's go to our library and read about it in *The Guidebook to Grammar Galaxy*."

Later, Kirk read the entry on humor aloud for his family.

Humor
Humor is a device used to make people smile, laugh, and enjoy literature in all its forms. People are more likely to remember what they read, hear, or watch when humor is used. Some common ways of using humor in writing include: **Hyperbole** – Overstatement makes the audience feel superior. In the book *Kel Gilligan's Daredevil Stunt Show*, we read that Kel gets dressed by himself (without a net!). **Surprise** – The reader is led to expect one conclusion when another is presented.   In the movie *Up*, Dug says, "Hey, I know a joke! A squirrel walks up to a tree and says, "I forgot to store acorns for the winter and now I am dead." **Slapstick or physical comedy** – The audience feels superior to the character who fails. Thieves in the movie *Home Alone* are repeatedly injured but not killed, making the audience laugh. **Incongruity** – An unexpected pairing creates the surprise needed for humor. In *Monster's Inc.*, monsters are afraid of children. **Irony** – The audience knows something that makes the character's words or actions a mismatch. In the movie *Toy Story*, the dialogue uses irony. Woody: "You are a toy! You aren't the real Buzz Lightyear! You're – You're an action figure! You are a child's plaything!" Buzz: "You are a sad, strange little man, and you have my pity." **Sarcasm** – The meaning is the opposite of what is said. In the movie *Frozen*, Olaf calls the monster 'Marshmallow' though he isn't sweet or harmless. **Pun** – A joke that makes use of more than one meaning of a word. In the book *Amelia Bedelia*, the girl is asked to draw the drapes, meaning to close them. She sketches them instead. Overuse of puns outside of children's literature is frowned upon. Insulting jokes, including those based on stereotypes (unfounded beliefs about an entire group of people), should also be avoided.

"I know what hyperbole is. It's the greatest humor device ever!" Luke said, smirking.

"Right, Luke. Very funny," Kirk said sarcastically.

"*The Galaxy's Funniest Home Videos* host uses a lot of puns. I guess because so many kids watch it?" Ellen said.

The queen nodded. "I don't mind them," she said.

"I do," the king said. "But for now it's all we have to make us laugh. Except..." he said, looking around. "We have plenty of funny books in our library! The humor writers' strike doesn't change that. I'm sure you haven't read all of them."

The English children agreed that they hadn't read all the funny books they owned. "Why don't you three choose a book to read right now," the king suggested.

The king and queen enjoyed looking for humorous books for their children. Each child took a book to read before bed.

The next afternoon, Ellen found the queen in her study. "Mother, may I read you the story I wrote for my creative writing class?"

The queen stopped what she was doing. "By all means! I'd love to hear it," she said.

Ellen read it aloud:

Detective Robert

Ms. Fleming's wig has gone missing. My name is Robert Hemmingway and my dream is to be a detective. I go to Marshwood Elementary and I'm in the second grade. Ms. Fleming is my teacher and she is a cancer survivor. She wears her wig every single day. This morning, however, she wasn't wearing her wig. I assumed the obvious: Her wig was stolen!

I didn't want to make a big deal out of her not wearing her wig, so I didn't say anything to Ms. Fleming. Instead, I took a **subtle** approach. At recess, I gathered all the kids. Some I put on jury duty and some were the suspects. I, of course, was the judge.

First suspect: Ally. She puts up an act of being kind, sensitive, and compassionate. And she's always crying. What a joke!

Second suspect: Jake, the class bad boy. He doesn't wash his hands before eating, he won't trade his food, and he watches PG-13 movies.

Last suspect: Sage. She's the teacher's pet. I don't think she did it; I just don't like her.

After recess is over, the jury and I decide Sage is guilty.

I return from recess ready to tell Ms. Fleming my conclusion of who

---

took her wig. "Ms. Fleming, Sage was the one who stole your wig," I say, beaming with pride. Ms. Fleming looked confused. "Pardon me? My wig is right here. I took it off because it felt itchy."

"Oh, Ms. Fleming, I'm so sorry," I said sheepishly.

That was when I decided I didn't want to be a detective anymore.

"Ellen, that was so funny! I love your sense of humor. You used several humor elements that we learned about last night. You have to read it to your father," the queen said, beaming.

★ ★ ★ ★ ★ ★ ★ ★ ★ ★
subtle – *understated*
★ ★ ★ ★ ★ ★ ★ ★ ★ ★

After Ellen read the story to her father, he congratulated her on excellent humor writing. He hugged her and said, "Ellen, you've given me an idea for how we can get through this humor writers' strike. We need to get the guardians reading and watching the humorous material they have at home. But we also need to get them writing humor themselves! Would you find Kirk and Luke and ask them to help you write a mission?"

Ellen agreed and the three English children sent a mission called Humor.

What does *resolved* mean?

What is a pun?

What humor method was Ellen using when Ms. Fleming said she had her wig?

Unit II: Adventures in Spelling & Vocabulary

Chapter 9

Ellen's friend Cher was having dinner with the royal English family one Friday evening. She planned to sleep over. Ellen had been looking forward to the sleepover for weeks.

When the main meal was served, Cher's eyes grew wide. "This looks amazing!" she gushed. The king and queen chuckled, and the boys smiled. Luke liked Cher.

After taking a bite, Cher said, "It tastes amazing too!" The rest of the family agreed.

The king asked one of the servers to send their compliments to Cook. "Yes, tell her it's amazing!" Cher said, smiling broadly.

The server promised to **relay** the message.

★ ★ ★ ★ ★ ★ ★ ★ ★ ★

relay – *communicate*

★ ★ ★ ★ ★ ★ ★ ★ ★ ★

When dessert was served, the family wasn't disappointed in Cher's reaction. "It's..." she began.

"Amazing?" Luke suggested with a teasing smile.

"Yes! Exactly!" Cher agreed. But Ellen glowered at Luke. Luke shrugged to suggest his innocence.

After dinner, the girls prepared Comet for a walk. "You have the most amazing dog!" Cher cooed as she cuddled him. Ellen smiled and led the way to the royal gardens.

"El, this garden is totally amazing. I am literally in awe," Cher said as they started their walk.

"Thanks! The groundskeepers do an amazing job with it," Ellen answered. "They're literally out here every day taking care of it," she explained.

"That's amazing," Cher added. "Just like this amazing dog here," she said, scratching behind Comet's ears. "He literally loves this," she said, grinning.

The girls enjoyed a long walk and returned to the castle, wanting to watch a movie. "I'm literally okay with anything," Cher said as Ellen reviewed their options.

"Okay. What about *Princess Diaries*?" Ellen asked.

"That would be so amazing," Cher said.

Ellen went to get popcorn and **beverages** from the kitchen. Meanwhile, the queen popped into the media room to check on the girls. Cher explained that Ellen was getting a snack. "Your house is literally amazing," Cher told the queen.

★ ★ ★ ★ ★ ★ ★ ★ ★ ★
beverages – *drinks*
trepidation – *fear*
★ ★ ★ ★ ★ ★ ★ ★ ★ ★

"Thank you!" the queen said, beaming. The two chatted about Cher's family and a recent vacation they'd taken until Ellen returned.

"What movie are you watching?" the queen asked. When Ellen told her their choice, her eyes brightened. "Would you be okay with me joining you? I love that movie," she said.

When Cher said that she didn't mind at all, Ellen consented. "This is going to be amazing!" Cher said. "I'm watching a chick flick with the queen of Grammar Galaxy!" Ellen and her mother couldn't help but laugh at Cher's enthusiasm.

With some **trepidation**, the queen asked if she could invite Cook to join them. "She loves watching chick flicks," she explained.

The girls readily agreed, and the queen went to get Cook, who had a tray of freshly baked brownies with her.

"I thought we needed a little chocolate too," Cook said, grinning.

"You are so amazing!" Cher said, hugging Cook.

"Why, thank you!" Cook said, amused by their guest's show of affection and gratitude. She took a seat and the four of them enjoyed watching the movie together.

"I am literally so glad the boys weren't here to make fun of us," Ellen said.

The other three agreed as they dabbed at happy tears with tissue.

The family said goodbye to Cher the next day. They asked her to visit again any time and they meant it.

"She is an amazing friend," the queen said.

"Literally," Ellen agreed.

"Totally," Luke added.

Ellen turned to look at Luke to see if he was teasing her. "Literally! She's an amazing friend," he said, defending himself.

"Totally," Kirk agreed.

"Great grammar, that's it!" the king roared.

"What is it?" the queen asked, startled by his eruption.

"I like Cher, but I haven't heard anything but amazing, literally, and totally since she arrived," the king said.

"I totally don't think it's that bad," Ellen said.

"It literally isn't," Luke said.

"And Cher is pretty amazing, isn't she?" Kirk asked. Everyone but the king nodded.

The king sighed. "You don't see anything wrong with the way you're talking?" he asked.

When his family shrugged, the king led them to the library. He removed *The Guidebook to Grammar Galaxy* from its shelf. Then he read them the article entitled "Overused Words."

Overused Words
Repeating certain words in writing and speaking should be avoided. Written work can be shorter, more interesting, and better at sharing important information without these words.

Use a variety of vocabulary words instead of relying on the same few. Check a thesaurus to find better choices. A chart of some common overused words and alternatives follows.

Instead of...	Try...
amazing/awesome/great	phenomenal/spectacular/wonderful
totally	leaving it out
literally/actually/honestly/seriously	leaving them out
nice	fantastic/delightful/polite
was like	said/told
very/really	leaving them out

"That totally makes sense," Ellen said.

"But I think Cher is amazing just the way she is. Do we have to tell her to use more vocabulary words?" Kirk asked, frowning.

"No one is suggesting we be rude. We wouldn't want to correct Cher for her choice of words," the king said.

"But your father is right and amazing as always," the queen said, side hugging him. "We do want you children to have a broad vocabulary."

"Why did you say I was amazing?" the king asked.

"Because you are!" the queen said. "Literally."

"Did you hear what you said?" the king asked.

The queen gasped and her hand flew to her mouth. "I totally said an overused word. I'm so sorry, dear."

"You just did it again. At first, I thought this was a matter of you spending time with the amazing Cher...What on English? That settles it. Something else is totally going on here," the king said. "Screen, give me a status report on planet Vocabulary," he ordered.

"Your Majesty, I have nothing significant to report from the planet," Screen replied.

"There totally has to be," the king said. "Search again, will you?" he asked.

A more detailed search produced no news stories to explain the overused words.

Ellen brightened. "I have an amazing idea! Kirk, Luke, and I will go to planet Vocabulary to investigate. And here's an even more amazing idea: Cher can come with us! She could literally learn about overused words without us being rude."

The king stroked his beard thoughtfully. "That really is an amazing idea," he concluded.

"Right?" Ellen replied. "And how about this...when we discover the problem, we can send out a mission on overused words to the guardians."

The entire family agreed it was literally, a totally amazing idea. Cher's family agreed that she could accompany the three English children. They left for planet Vocabulary using the space porter.

What does *trepidation* mean?

What are some examples of overused words?

Why did the king suspect something was wrong on planet Vocabulary?

Chapter 10

"Children, we are going to visit your grandfather in his new home today," the queen announced at breakfast. "He has just moved into an assisted-living apartment."

"What does that mean—*assisted-living*?" Luke asked.

"It means that he has someone helping him get around. He still can't walk since his hip surgery. They give him his meals and do his laundry and cleaning. They have entertainment there too," the queen explained.

"He seems to be enjoying it," the king said. "But he is eager to see us."

The three English children loved their Grandpa George and looked forward to the visit.

The royal family arrived at the apartment after lunch. Grandpa George was beaming when the five of them walked in.

"This is beautiful!" Ellen said, hugging him.

"Yeah, it's a cool apartment, Grandpa," Luke said.

"Thank you. Gimme some skin, boys," their grandpa said, holding out his hand. The two boys looked to their father, confused.

"He wants you to shake his hand," the king said, laughing.

The boys chuckled too and shook their grandfather's hand.

"You're looking foxy," Grandpa George told his daughter, the queen. She blushed and hugged him.

Ellen looked alarmed. *Why would Grandpa say Mother looked like a fox?* she wondered. *And why did she seem happy he had said it?*

"Of course, I was happier when my old lady was with me," Grandpa George said, tearing up, "but I'm making new friends."

"That's so good to hear," the queen said, looking misty herself. "I miss Mother so much."

What old lady? Kirk wondered. *Does he mean Grandma?*

"I spend time here hanging loose, but I enjoy going to the dining hall and activity center. Do you want to see it?" Grandpa George asked.

Everyone agreed enthusiastically. *What did Grandpa allow to hang loose?* Luke wondered. He looked to see if his shirt was untucked, but it wasn't.

The queen began pushing her father's wheelchair toward the door when he stopped her. "I have to get myself around as long as I'm able. Can you dig it?"

The queen stopped pushing the chair and apologized. "Of course," she said.

Grandpa George smiled and led the way down to the hall to the elevator.

What did Mother need to dig for Grandpa? Ellen wondered. *Did he have flowers he wanted to be planted?* Ellen walked near her mother and grandfather as they exited the elevator.

"How are you doing without your mother around?" Grandpa asked the queen. "Lay it on me."

"Do you want a blanket, Grandfather? I can go back and get you one," Ellen suggested.

Grandpa George looked at her quizzically. "No, but it's very kind of you to offer," he said, patting Ellen on the hand.

The queen responded to her father's question by saying she was more worried about him.

"I'm not trying to be heavy," he reassured her.

Grandpa didn't seem overweight, but I guess he is watching what he eats? Ellen thought.

"I know you're not," the queen reassured him.

"I'm okay. I just want you to be too," he said.

"I am," the queen said, rubbing his shoulder affectionately.

"Good then. Boys, you're gonna love this place," he announced loudly. "It's far out!"

Kirk wanted to ask how far, but he didn't want to upset his mother. He was surprised when the dining hall was a very short walk from his grandfather's building.

The room was lined with windows and was decorated like a fancy restaurant. **Ornate** chandeliers hung from the ceiling and fresh-floral centerpieces **adorned** the

★ ★ ★ ★ ★ ★ ★ ★ ★ ★
ornate – *fancy*
adorned – *decorated*
★ ★ ★ ★ ★ ★ ★ ★ ★

cloth-covered tables. "It's gorgeous!" Ellen exclaimed.

"I told you," Grandpa George said. "The food is marvelous too. This place costs some bread, but it's worth it. Fortunately, they have exercise classes, or I would be putting on some pounds," he said, patting his belly.

He IS worried about getting too heavy, Ellen thought. *Does he have to give them bread in order to eat here?* she wondered.

"Now I want to show you my favorite room of the whole place," Grandpa George said. He rolled his wheelchair in the direction of the **adjoining** hallway and the family followed.

★ ★ ★ ★ ★ ★ ★ ★ ★ ★
adjoining – *connecting*
★ ★ ★ ★ ★ ★ ★ ★ ★

"This is the game room," he said as they entered a room with a huge video screen and a number of gaming tables. "We can play ping pong, pool, and yes, even video games!" he exclaimed.

"Wow!" Luke exclaimed.

"Yes, it's a real gas," Grandpa George agreed.

"Gas? Do they have a gas leak in here?" Kirk asked, looking around worriedly.

The king and queen and Grandpa George laughed. "No, Kirk. It's fine," the queen said, patting him on the shoulder. "Why don't you three play a game with your grandfather?" she suggested.

Grandpa George and the kids played a video game on the big screen. The king and queen enjoyed watching them.

After some time, Grandpa George asked staff members to bring them some snacks. The kids thoroughly enjoyed them.

The family ended their visit with Grandpa George by walking the trail around the small lake on the property. "I knew this was the right place for you," the queen said, as they walked back to her father's apartment.

"Well, you were right," Grandpa George agreed. "You don't have to worry about me. But you do have to visit me again. I love seeing you and your beautiful family."

The queen teared up, hugged her father, and encouraged the kids to say their goodbyes.

On the way home, the king said how happy he was to see his father-in-law doing so well. The queen agreed. "I'm relieved. I didn't know how he would get along without Mother and not being in his own home," the queen said.

Kirk observed his parents' happiness about the visit. He debated whether to voice his concerns. He finally decided to mention what he'd noticed. "Is it possible that Grandpa George has dementia? I know it's not unusual at his age."

"What's dementia?" Luke asked.

"It's a condition affecting the brain that causes memory problems and confusion," Kirk said.

The queen was immediately concerned. Had her father said something to Kirk that she hadn't heard? "Why do you say that, Kirk? What did Grandpa say that worried you?" she asked him.

"Remember when he said the place we were going was far out when it was actually close? And then he said there was a gas leak in the game room when there wasn't," Kirk said.

Before the king and queen could respond, Ellen added, "And he called you a fox, Mother, and said he wanted you to lay it on him. But then he said he didn't want a blanket."

The king and queen looked at one another and laughed. They laughed so hard that the king was panting, and the queen was nearly in tears.

"What's so funny?" Kirk asked. He couldn't believe that his parents didn't take possible dementia seriously.

"Kirk, Grandpa doesn't have dementia," the queen said, laughing again. "He—, he just talks the way people his age talk."

The king tried to control himself. "I do think he was talking that way more than usual, don't you, dear?" he asked the queen.

The queen stopped laughing and thought. "You know, I think you're right."

"Children, in all seriousness, I just realized that we haven't taught you something important. Your grandfather was using slang," the king explained.

"Is it an old foreign language?" Kirk asked.

"No. It's English. I'll explain when we can use the guidebook at home," the king said, catching the queen's eye and laughing again.

The royal family arrived at home and settled into the media room. The king then had *The Guidebook to Grammar Galaxy* brought to him.

"This is slang," the king said, reading the entry aloud.

Slang
Slang is informal, usually spoken, language used by a particular group of people. It is used to help group members feel connected by assigning new meanings to words that only they understand. Slang includes acronyms used by a group. Youth create slang to demonstrate separateness from their parents' generation. For example, young Western women in the 1920s called new things they liked "the cat's pajamas." See the chart below for common slang from previous generations. **Jargon** is a form of slang often used within professional groups. For example, the term *pro se* (for someone who represents himself or herself in court without a lawyer) is legal jargon. **Portmanteau slang** is a slang word that is a combination of two words. (A portmanteau is a suitcase that opens like a book with a container on each side.) For example, *ginormous* is portmanteau slang. It is from *gigantic* and *enormous*, meaning huge. *Frenemy* is portmanteau slang for someone who is both a friend and enemy. To be certain of the meaning of slang, consult a slang dictionary.

Slang	Meaning
Far out	Fantastic
Wallflower	A shy person
Don't have a cow	Calm down
Ride	Car
A gas	Good time
Lay it on me	Tell me
Give me some skin	Shake hands or high-five
Gimme some sugar	Kiss me
Heavy	Serious
Foxy	Gorgeous
Old lady	Wife/girlfriend
Hang loose	Relaxing
Can you dig it?	Do you understand?
Groovy	Wonderful

"What's the difference between an idiom and slang?" Kirk asked when his father had finished reading.

"Excellent question, Kirk. An idiom is generally understood by everyone in a culture and idioms are frequently written. Slang is only understood by certain groups of people and isn't used in more formal writing. Jargon is used in formal writing but usually by members of a professional group."

"Wouldn't everyone understand each other better if we didn't use slang?" Ellen asked.

"Probably," the queen answered. "But we can't stop people from using it. Instead, we can try to learn slang, so we can understand the people we care about."

Ellen nodded. "I have an idea. I think we should send out a mission on slang to the guardians. Maybe their grandparents use slang too," she said.

"What a groovy idea!" the queen exclaimed.

"Yeah, far out, Ellen!" Kirk said, smirking.

The rest of the family laughed. The three English children got to work on a mission called Slang.

What does *adjoining* mean?

What's an example of slang you didn't know?

Why do you think Grandpa George isn't living with his wife?

Chapter II

Kirk was eager to open the envelope he received from Orange Industries when it arrived. He was sure it was approval of his application for the position of Robotics Apprentice.

But his countenance fell as he read. "We regret to inform you that you don't meet our qualifications for Robotics Apprentice at this time. We do, however, encourage you to apply again in the future."

Kirk was shocked. He thought he was guaranteed to get the position. He threw the letter down on the entry table in disgust. He went to his bedchamber **fuming**.

★ ★ ★ ★ ★ ★ ★ ★ ★ ★
fuming – *furious*
★ ★ ★ ★ ★ ★ ★ ★ ★ ★

The king found the letter on his way to the kitchen. He was surprised housekeeping hadn't picked it up. He glanced at it and noticed it was for Kirk. As he read, he frowned. No wonder the letter had been left there. *He must be so disappointed,* the king thought. He didn't know if he should discuss it with his son or not.

He took the letter to the kitchen with him and found Cook taking a fresh batch of cookies from the oven. "I'd like to take some of these to Kirk to cheer him up," he said, helping himself first.

"Why does he need cheering up?" Cook asked.

The king explained that he hadn't been accepted as an apprentice.

"Poor **lad**," Cook said. "I can't imagine anyone more qualified."

"Right," the king agreed.

★ ★ ★ ★ ★ ★ ★ ★ ★

lad – *boy*
snide – *sarcastic*

★ ★ ★ ★ ★ ★ ★ ★ ★

Later, Kirk accepted the plate of cookies from his father gratefully. His father held up the letter and told him he was sorry.

"I just don't understand it. I described all the projects I've done and mentioned our robotics team championship," Kirk said.

The king was upset by Kirk's discouragement. "This disappointment doesn't mean you aren't talented, Kirk," the king said. Kirk nodded that he understood. But he was still unhappy.

The king left Kirk to his cookies and made his way to his office. He was getting more and more annoyed by what he suspected was going on. Orange Industries didn't want to choose Kirk for the position and risk looking like they were trying to earn the king's favor. The more he thought about it, the more upset he got. He was going to give them a call.

He asked Screen to contact the director who had signed Kirk's letter. Soon he was on a video call with him. "Your Majesty, to what do I owe the honor of your call?" the man asked.

"I wanted to talk with you about the apprenticeship position my son Kirk applied for," the king said.

"Ah, yes. Kirk is an impressive young man. You must be so proud," the director said. "We were sorry we couldn't offer him the position this time around."

"Because it wouldn't look good to give the position to the king's son?" the king asked in a **snide** tone.

The director was startled. "No, no, not at all. That isn't why we didn't accept Kirk's application," he said.

"Why then?" the king challenged him.

63

The director sighed and continued reluctantly. "It's because of his logic exam score."

"Logic exam? What kind of logic exam?"

"We gave our applicants word analogies to complete. Every applicant this year failed. We are hoping that next year's pool of applicants does better. In fact, we would love to have your leadership in promoting logic education."

The king reddened in embarrassment and anger. But he took a breath so he wouldn't say what he was thinking. "I see. I will work for better logic education, beginning immediately. I'm hopeful the next set of test scores will be acceptable," the king said calmly.

"Thank you so much for your help and understanding, Your Majesty. We look forward to getting Kirk's application next year."

The king ended the call with a smile, but he was mad. How had they failed to teach word analogies? He would waste no time teaching his own children. He contacted them via their communicators and asked them to meet him in the castle library.

"What's the emergency?" Luke asked when they had all gathered. "Is the Gremlin on the attack again?"

"No, Luke. I'm afraid this is my own failing. I haven't taught you three about word analogies." He removed *The Guidebook to Grammar Galaxy* from the bookshelf and read them the entry on the topic.

Word Analogies
Word analogies, or verbal analogies, are often included in standardized tests. Solving word analogies, or determining the relationship between words, is a test of vocabulary and logic or reasoning. Verbal analogies are written in this format: **up:down::fast:slow** This analogy is read as "Up is to down as fast is to slow." To determine a missing word in an analogy, determine the relationship between the first word pair. Then apply that relationship to the second set of words. Choose the most likely word for the blank. **Rug:floor::painting:_____**

In this analogy, we determine that the floor is where a rug is placed. To complete the analogy, we ask where a painting is placed. The answer is *wall*.

"I admit I hadn't seen word pairs like that before," Kirk said. "But I guessed correctly what a word analogy was. Like *word* is to *sentence* as *page* is to *wagon*." Kirk wasn't happy when he saw the look on his father's face.

"Kirk, it wouldn't be *page* is to *wagon*. It would be *page* is to *wagon*." The king gasped when he realized what he'd said. "Something is wrong," he said.

"I knew it!" Kirk said gleefully. "It's not me."

The king asked Screen to give him any news from planet Vocabulary. "This is all I have, Your Majesty," Screen replied. It was an advertisement for a series of talks by Dr. Wordlove.

"The galaxy's leading expert on word relationships helps words find their soulmates," the ad read.

"Do you have any more information on these seminars?" the king asked Screen. Soon a video played of word pairs leaving an auditorium together. Scrolling underneath was the tagline "Another Dr. Wordlove match."

"Those words don't go together!" Luke exclaimed.

"Correct, Luke. That's what's causing the problem," the king said. "I'm going to find out what Dr. Wordlove's qualifications are. My guess is she isn't a doctor at all. The Gremlin is likely paying her."

"You can get Dr. Wordlove or whoever she is to stop matching the wrong words. But how are we going to get the words that have already been matched into the right relationships?" Ellen asked.

"Good question," Luke said.

"You know what I just noticed?" Kirk said. "How much Mother looks like Dr. Wordlove. We could go to planet Vocabulary and find the word pairs that she's matched. Then we can get the guardians to help us make the right matches. Mother can tell them that she has an even better match for them. The words would assume she was Dr. Wordlove."

"That's brilliant, Kirk," the king said. Luke and Ellen agreed.

The family had the queen come to the library so they could explain. She loved the idea of being a doctor for a day. Once they assessed the situation on planet Vocabulary, the English children planned to send the guardians a mission called Word Analogies.

What does *fuming* mean?

What is the first step in solving a word analogy?

Why were Kirk and the king giving the wrong answer to the analogy **word:sentence::page:_____?**

Chapter 12

One evening after the queen finished reading to the family, she had a thought. "The year 3000 is nearly here. It's a special year. We ought to have a galaxy-wide celebration," she **mused** aloud.

"This is going to cost me money," the king groaned.

The queen chuckled. "We should **splurge** on such an important occasion."

"What are you thinking, Mother?" Ellen asked, sharing her excitement.

"I was thinking we ought to have a masquerade ball," the queen said.

Ellen squealed with delight. "So we'll be here at the castle at midnight? In costume? We'll need to have costumes made."

"See? I told you it was going to cost me," the king grumbled.

"We should have fireworks," Kirk added.

"Those are expensive too, but I agree, Kirk. We'll have a fireworks display," the king said.

Kirk smiled gratefully.

"Let's talk about the most important part," Luke said. When his family asked what he meant, he replied, "Food, of course. What are we having?" Everyone laughed.

"Very good point, Luke. I'll need to talk with Cook about the menu," the queen said.

In the following weeks, the family and castle staff kept very busy making plans for the year-end celebration. Leaders on all the planets were occupied with party planning as well.

With a week left before the celebration, Kirk knocked on his father's office door. "Come in," the king said pleasantly. When he saw it was Kirk, he welcomed him warmly. "What's on your mind, son? Are we ready to go with the fireworks display?"

"We are," Kirk said. "It's going to be the greatest display the galaxy's ever had."

"I know you're excited. Truth be told, I am too. I love fireworks. The costume ball I could do without, but it's important to your mother." He paused waiting for Kirk to tell him what he was thinking about.

"I did something you asked me not to do," Kirk said hesitantly.

"All right, I'm listening," the king said, a little worried.

"I've been reading computer hacker forums online. I know there could be people there who want my personal information. But I haven't posted in the forums. I also know there could be adult content on the forums that I shouldn't be reading," Kirk continued.

"That's right. There could be," the king said soberly. "Go on."

"I want you to forgive me for disobeying you."

"I do forgive you, Kirk. I appreciate you telling me too. Please don't read the forums anymore. If you want to learn from other programmers, you can talk with our head programmer. You can ask him what the hot topics are."

"I know. But there's something else..." Kirk said.

"Okay," the king said with some trepidation.

"I saw a lot of chatter about computer viruses being unleashed when the year changes to 3000," Kirk said.

"Couldn't it just be talk?" the king asked. "The new year is all anyone is talking about."

"I don't think so. I'm concerned that Prefix and Suffix may be behind the hacking."

"What? That would be just like them to try to ruin the happy occasion." The king sighed and stroked his beard. "I want you to go with me to talk with our head programmer." Kirk agreed and the two went to find him.

The head programmer was seated at his computer in his office and rose to greet the two royals when they came in. Kirk told him what he had read on the forums and his concerns about Prefix and Suffix.

The programmer nodded and listened **intently**. "I've heard this too," he said.

★ ★ ★ ★ ★ ★ ★ ★ ★
intently – *closely*
★ ★ ★ ★ ★ ★ ★ ★ ★

"You have? Why haven't you consulted me?" the king asked, his voice rising.

The programmer motioned for the king to calm down. "Because I don't think there's any reason to worry. In fact, I think that's their plan. They get us all worried that our systems will shut down at midnight. Then we can't enjoy the celebration."

"Hm. You make a good point," the king said, thinking for a moment. "But if we're wrong, we're in trouble. I think it would be wise to do some investigating. I don't want Kirk to be exposed to the dark side of the web. Know what I mean?"

The programmer nodded.

"But I do want you to work together on this. I want to know if there are computer viruses in the works."

"Yes, Your Majesty," the programmer agreed. Kirk was beaming and thanked his father.

When the king left, the programmer invited Kirk to sit. "I think I know where we can look for any secret activity."

A few days later, the king went to check on their progress. "Do you think it's a credible threat?" he asked the programmer.

"At this point, no. Several people I trust are saying it's just talk. They don't think there's any way a hacker could bring our system down. We've made multiple improvements in system security since the last attack we had."

"That's reassuring," the king said, brightening. "I'm still glad you've checked into it," he said, directing his words to Kirk.

"Thanks for allowing me to help, Father," Kirk said. "I appreciate your confidence in me."

The morning of New Year's Eve, the king received a call from Grammar Patrol on planet Vocabulary. "I apologize for disturbing you on a holiday, Your Highness, but I see some unusual activity here," the captain said.

"Go on," the king urged him.

"A number of prefixes, suffixes, and root words are gathering in the public square."

"Getting ready for the New Year's celebration?" the king asked.

"That's what I thought at first. But they're lining up, almost like, almost like..."

"Yes?" the king encouraged him to continue.

69

"Almost like they're going to war."

"What?" the king shrieked. "That can't be possible."

"I could be wrong, but it doesn't look right. And most of my officers are off for the holiday. I thought you'd want to know."

"Of course," the king said, thanking him for his report. He had no time to think about this news before Kirk burst into his office.

"Father, I don't think our computer systems are at risk. I think we're on the brink of civil war," he said breathlessly. "Someone who is loyal to the galaxy sent me a secret document. It has a list of prefixes, suffixes, and root words that are serving with the Gremlin resistance. Here," he said handing his father the list. The king read over the list.

Prefixes	Definition	Examples
anti-	against, opposite	antivirus, antibiotic
en-, em-	to cause, to put or go into	enable, embark
centi-	hundred	centimeter, centipede
deca-, deci	ten	decade, decimal
fore-	before	forewarned, foreword
milli-, mille- kilo-	thousand	millimeter, millennium, kilogram
multi-, poly-	many	multiple, polygon
semi-	half	semicolon, semicircle
sub-	under, below, secondary	submerge, substandard

Suffixes	Definition	Examples
-able, -ible	can be done	likable, sensible
-an	having skill, relating or belonging to	electrician, American
-ance, -ence	act, condition	excellence, importance
-ive	like, likely to act	sensitive, active

Roots	Definition	Examples
ject	throw	projectile, inject
jur, juris	judge, law	jury, jurisdiction
mit	send	transmit, admit
path	feel, suffer, disease	sympathy, pathology
struct	build	construct, instruct

"With these prefixes, suffixes, and root words opposing us, we are facing disaster," the king said gravely.

"What do we do?" Kirk asked.

"We have to assemble our own army."

"You mean we're going to war with our own words?" Kirk asked.

"Just as a means to get them to surrender, Kirk. We can't afford to ignore them." Kirk nodded that he understood. "We need Luke and Ellen and all the guardians to help us. There is no time to waste."

The three English children worked with their father to send an emergency mission to the guardians. They called it Prefixes, Suffixes, and Root Words. They didn't want to upset the guardians by calling the mission Civil War. They also didn't tell the queen, hoping they could resolve the crisis by that evening.

What does *mused* mean?

Which of these prefixes, suffixes, and root words do you think are most dangerous in a war?

Why didn't the king want Kirk going on hacker forums online?

Chapter 13

One evening the king and queen sat in the media room after the children had gone to bed. The queen was reading, and the king was watching the late-night news. The queen was so captivated by her book that she didn't protest as she normally did. She did not like hearing bad news before she went to sleep.

"This is an outrage!" the king exclaimed.

The queen was startled enough to look up from her book. "What is it now?" she asked with no small amount of irritation.

"I didn't think even the Gremlin would go so far," the king said. When the queen shrugged as if to say 'explain it to me,' he continued. "Apostrophes are going to be rounded up and **evicted** from planet Spelling," the king said. His neck and face were becoming **crimson** with anger.

★ ★ ★ ★ ★ ★ ★ ★ ★ ★

evicted– *removed*
crimson– *red*
ushered– *guided*

★ ★ ★ ★ ★ ★ ★ ★ ★ ★

"Well, they can't do that, can they?" the queen said.

"They're doing it! Look!" the king said, pointing at the screen. Large numbers of apostrophes were being **ushered** onto buses.

"Where are they taking them?" the queen asked.

"To some detention center," the king said sadly.

"Why? What have they done wrong?"

"They are considered imposters. They're not letters, so the governing authorities there want them out."

"Planet Spelling should be open to punctuation too," the queen said.

"It should be, but it isn't right now," the king said. "We have a crisis on our hands."

"What are you going to do? There must be hundreds of apostrophes that have been removed," the queen said.

"It's too late to get the guardians involved now. But first thing in the morning, I'll talk to the children," the king said.

The next day, the king read the article in the *Grammar Gazette* on what was being called the Impostor Apostrophes Crisis. He was even more upset than he had been the night before. When Kirk, Luke, and Ellen joined him in the dining room for breakfast, he stood.

"I'm sorry, children, but you're going to have to delay breakfast. There is an emergency on planet Spelling that can't wait," he said.

"Something on planet Spelling is more important than breakfast?" Luke complained. He stopped when he saw his father's expression. "Okay, what is it?" he asked.

The king answered him by asking Screen to play a video report on the removal of apostrophes from the planet. A small crowd of protestors was gathered, holding signs that read "No impostors allowed." Apostrophes were being loaded onto buses and driven away.

"Where are they taking the apostrophes?" Ellen asked, sympathizing with them.

"To a detainment camp somewhere on the planet. I'm afraid the next stop will be planet Recycling," he said gravely.

"What's a detainment camp?" Luke asked.

"A place where they are being held against their will," the king said.

Another video played on the screen. Two political commentators were discussing the apostrophe crisis. "I think we need to be honest here and admit that apostrophes aren't letters. Because they aren't, they cause a lot of confusion on planet Spelling," one man said.

"But haven't they always lived on planet Spelling?" the woman sitting opposite him asked.

"Yes, and there has always been a lot of confusion on the planet," the first commentator responded.

The woman nodded. "Will spelling be better without the apostrophe? And what is the future of the apostrophes who are being forced to leave the planet? Join us for more after this message from our sponsor," the woman said.

"I can tell you the answers to those questions!" the king roared. "Spelling will be more confusing, not less. And if the Gremlin has his way, those apostrophes will be destroyed. We have to do something to save them."

The king called for *The Guidebook to Grammar Galaxy* to be brought to him. When it arrived, he said, "We've forgotten the important role the apostrophe plays in spelling. We have to educate our planet about them. But first, we have to educate ourselves." The king read the entry on apostrophes aloud.

Apostrophes

An apostrophe is a punctuation mark (') used to show possession, omission of letters as in contractions, or the plural of letters and numbers.

Apostrophes are used after the noun that possesses something. If a plural noun ends in s, the apostrophe follows the s.

The dog's mouth was covered in mud. – *correct*

Two dog's owners picked up their pets from the groomer. – *incorrect*; the apostrophe goes after the s.

Its, his, hers, ours, and yours are possessive pronouns that end in s. They do not use apostrophes.

Its wounded paw caused the dog to limp. – *correct*

The purse left in the café was her's. – *incorrect*

Apostrophes are used to form contractions or to indicate missing letters or numbers.

It's time to go! – *correct*; the apostrophe stands for the *i* in *it is*

Your going to be late. – *incorrect*; use *you're* which stands for you are.

Life was much different in the '50s. – *correct*; the apostrophe takes the place of 19 in 1950s.

An apostrophe and an s form the plural for single letters and numbers. Apostrophes with an s do not form other plurals.

Does anyone have any 5's? – *correct*

Be sure to dot your is and cross your ts. – *incorrect*

My mother is having lunch with other mom's. – *incorrect*

The king showed his children the last example in the guidebook. "What's that word?" he asked with his finger under the i-s.

"It looks like *is* to me," Luke said.

"Precisely! That's why we need the apostrophe there. Otherwise, the plural of the letter *i* looks like *is*," the king said.

"Won't the removal of apostrophes from the planet cause contraction confusion?" Kirk asked.

"Exactly, Kirk," the king said. "We have apostrophes on the planet to prevent confusion, not cause it," he added.

"What can we do?" Ellen asked.

"I want you children to get the guardians on a campaign to save the apostrophes. Teach them why they matter in the galaxy. Have them do whatever they can to create sympathy for this punctuation mark."

"And we need to go on a rescue mission too, don't we?" Luke asked hopefully.

The king smiled. "Yes. I want you three to go to planet Spelling and find out where the apostrophes are being held. I'll send you with a royal order for them to be released immediately. The guardians can help you get them home."

The three English children worked on a mission called Apostrophes. And they made plans to leave for planet Spelling as soon as they finished breakfast.

What does *crimson* mean?

What's one important job an apostrophe does?

What did protestors call the apostrophes?

Chapter 14

"You seem worried, dear," the queen said one evening as the royal couple prepared for bed.

"Not worried exactly, more concerned," the king said. He chuckled when he realized that worry and concern were nearly the same thing. "Here's my concern. I have seen a marked decline in spelling in recent years. We have taught the guardians many strategies for spelling, but I think I need to take more serious action."

"Like what?" the queen asked.

"Like hiring a consultant to help."

"That's a splendid idea! It's like how I kept trying to improve my cooking by watching shows and reading cookbooks. I didn't get the results I wanted until I asked Cook to coach me."

"Exactly!" the king said. "Sometimes we need a fresh **perspective** on a problem. You've convinced me to call the consultant that was recommended to me. I'll call first thing in the morning. But you'll always be my best grammar gal," the king said, kissing his wife on the cheek.

★ ★ ★ ★ ★ ★ ★ ★ ★ ★

perspective – *viewpoint*

★ ★ ★ ★ ★ ★ ★ ★ ★ ★

"And I thought you weren't a romantic," the queen said teasingly.

A few days later, the king found his wife in her office. He was brimming with enthusiasm. "My new consultant has a galaxy-wide campaign to improve spelling up and running," the king said. "He believes it will encourage teamwork on planet Spelling. That will, in turn, create better spellers on planet English."

"I love the idea of teamwork!" the queen exclaimed.

"Yes, I do too," the king agreed. "The consultant believes we should see improvements in spelling very quickly."

"Luke will be especially happy to hear this news," the queen said.

The next morning the king sat reading his paper at the dining room table. "What on English?" he roared.

"Dear, lower your voice," the queen encouraged him. "The children are still sleeping."

"This is an outrage!" the king continued, ignoring the queen's **admonition**.

★ ★ ★ ★ ★ ★ ★ ★ ★ ★
admonition – *caution*
superfluous – *excessive*
★ ★ ★ ★ ★ ★ ★ ★ ★ ★

"What on English is wrong?" the queen asked.

"I'll tell you what's wrong. Look at this paper," the king said, showing her the front page of the *Grammar Gazette*.

"Oh my!" the queen exclaimed. "Why are there so many hyphens?"

"Why indeed," the king said angrily. "I am going to get to the bottom of this right now, even though it's early."

The king marched out of the dining room, determined to reach the editor of the newspaper.

"To what do I owe the pleasure?" the editor asked upon seeing the king on his screen.

"I'm afraid it isn't going to be a pleasure at all," the king said, holding up the front page of the paper. "What is the meaning of this?"

"I'm not sure what you mean," the editor said hesitantly.

"The hyphens, obviously," the king said.

"Yes, we are hyphenating words as part of your Better Together campaign. I spoke at length with your consultant, who assured me that this was a part of your plan to improve spelling.

"That's preposterous!" The king said so loudly that the editor jumped. "I told my consultant no such thing. Hyphens were never discussed."

"I see," the editor said with a tight smile. "Am I to assume that you are canceling the Better Together spelling campaign?"

"That is a safe assumption. I better not see this **superfluous** hyphenation in tomorrow's issue. Am I clear?"

"Completely. However, might I suggest that you speak with your consultant?" the editor said snidely.

78

The king wanted to respond in kind but simply said he would be talking with his consultant.

The king couldn't wait to find out what was going on. He asked Screen to contact his consultant. Screen reported that he was not answering the call. "Do your best to locate him," the king barked. "I have to speak to him now."

"I am not getting a location for him, Your Majesty. He must have his location blocked," Screen reported.

"Of course he does," the king said. "I've been tricked," he said, sighing.

The king returned to the dining room, where the children were having breakfast with the queen. "I'm afraid I have bad news," he told them. He showed them the hyphenated newspaper and explained that his consultant was responsible. "I hired him to improve spelling and this is the result," he said bitterly.

"What can we do to help?" Kirk asked, sympathizing with his father.

"I will do what I can to have the Better Together campaign halted. But I will need you children to go to planet Spelling. You will have to separate the hyphens from words where they don't belong."

"All these hyphens?" Luke asked, pulling the newspaper toward him.

"I'm afraid so, Luke. You'll need the guardians' help and you'll need to learn the rules for using hyphens." The king asked for *The Guidebook to Grammar Galaxy* to be brought in. He read them the entry on hyphens when it arrived.

Hyphens
The word *hyphen* is from the Greek for *together*. Hyphens (-) are used to create some compound words. Note that compound words often begin as separate words. They then become hyphenated and finally become closed compound words with no hyphen. Check a dictionary to determine if a compound word requires a hyphen. **Some examples of hyphenated compound words are** check-in, check-up, Commander-in-Chief, President-Elect, mother-in-law, self-esteem, runner-up, singer-songwriter, jack-in-the-box, blue-green, merry-go-round, go-between, pick-me-up, good-for-nothing, two-year-old.

Hyphenate two or more words that describe the following noun. This is called a compound adjective. To determine if it should be hyphenated, ask if each word makes sense describing the noun alone. If not, the words should be hyphenated. Adjective phrases that begin with an -ly adverb and those formed by proper nouns should not be hyphenated.

She was going on a once-in-a-lifetime trip. — *Correct*

The trip was out-of-this-world — Incorrect, adjectives follow the noun

That really-moldy doll should be thrown out. — *Incorrect*

The Red-Star guardian got to work. *Incorrect*

Her easy-come-easy-go approach to life causes problems. — Correct

His my way or the highway attitude causes problems. — *Incorrect; it isn't my attitude or highway attitude, so the words my-way-or-the-highway should be hyphenated.*

Hyphens are also used to continue words that are split at the end of a line. The hyphen must appear between syllables. Check a dictionary if you aren't sure where to hyphenate a word.

Her favorite vocabulary word is *sen-sational. — Correct*

His friend's family is thinking about ho-meschooling. — *Incorrect*

"Let me get this straight," Luke said. "We have to remove hyphens from words where they don't belong."

The king nodded.

"And we're going to have to use a dictionary to look up compound words."

"I'm afraid so," the king agreed.

"Hyphens can also be included in compound adjectives," Luke continued.

"And when words are split at the end of a line," Ellen interjected.

Luke sighed. "This is going to be a lot of work."

"It is. But I trust you and the guardians to get the job done," the king said.

The three English children finished their breakfast and used the newspaper to create a mission called Hyphens. Then they used the space porter to travel to planet Sentence.

What does *admonition* mean?

At the end of a line, hyphens should go between what?

Why were there so many hyphens in the newspaper?

Chapter 15

The king received a phone call from the Prime Minister one afternoon. The Prime Minister wasted no time giving the king the reason for his call.

"Your Highness, I wanted to give you notice of a bill being debated in Parliament," he said.

"Yes, what is it?" the king asked without particular concern.

"They're calling it the Word Opportunity for Employment Act," the Prime Minister said.

"The acronym is WOE? That's funny," the king said, chuckling.

"Yes, well, it's a bit of a whoa as well as a woe, if you know what I mean," he answered.

"What does the bill say?" the king asked.

"The bill allows words to be spelled the same way, regardless of their part of speech. Words are to be given equal opportunity in spelling," he explained.

The king laughed. "You must be joking! Is it April Fools' Day? That's a good one," he said.

"I'm afraid I'm not joking," the Prime Minister said. "What's worse is I believe there is broad support for the bill."

"I won't give my **assent**," the king said.

"I'm afraid it isn't that simple," the Prime Minister warned.

★ ★ ★ ★ ★ ★ ★ ★ ★ ★

assent – *agreement*
apprised – *informed*
replete – *full*

★ ★ ★ ★ ★ ★ ★ ★ ★ ★

"What do you mean?"

"Polls are suggesting that nearly three-quarters of the people are in favor of it," the Prime Minister said.

"People have been polled, but it hasn't been discussed with me!" the king complained. "So, if I don't agree to it, then what?"

"You'll likely have protests. And your approval rating could drop to a record low," he warned.

"Approval ratings aren't my concern, Mr. Prime Minister. My job is to protect the English language. If this bill becomes law, there will be confusion. I can't allow that," the king said.

"I understand, Your Majesty," the Prime Minister said. "I just wanted you to know what you're up against."

The two said their goodbyes after the Prime Minister promised to keep the king **apprised** of the bill's progress.

The king asked the screen in his office to research the Word Opportunity for Employment Act. He wasn't surprised by what he found. The Internet was **replete** with ads discussing the unfairness words faced with spelling. The ads blamed the king for the injustice. Every ad was sponsored by an organization called The Center for Word Liberty.

The king asked Screen to show him more information about the organization. Their website description read "The Center for Word Liberty is dedicated to lobbying for words' freedom, regardless of a word's part of speech. We educate the public about laws that threaten words' pursuit of happiness."

"Of course!" the king said to himself. "The Gremlin is behind this organization. They're convincing members of Parliament that we need this law to protect words. They're fooling the public with these misleading ads."

The king thought for a while about how to respond. He summoned his butler and asked him to have his family gather in the library.

"You know I don't like politics," he began when they arrived. "But sometimes it's necessary to get involved to protect this galaxy. I have reason to believe that the Gremlin has been lobbying Parliament to pass a dangerous law."

"What law?" Kirk asked.

"It's called the Word Opportunity for Employment Act or WOE, which is just silly," the king said.

"Oh, I saw an ad for that when I was playing Stardust," Luke said.

"I know the Gremlin is behind it, but do you think the law could be a good idea? It might be easier for words to have the same spellings," Kirk said.

The king sighed. "The unique spellings help us determine the meaning of the words and their parts of speech. They make English less confusing, not more. Let me read to you from the guidebook," he said, removing *The Guidebook to Grammar Galaxy* from the shelf.

"You remember what homophones are, correct?" the king asked as he paged through the guidebook.

"Yes!" Ellen said. "*Homo-* means same and *phon* means sound. So homophones are words that sound the same but are different."

"Correct. They can be spelled the same as homographs are, or they can be spelled differently," the king said.

"Right, like *eye* the eye I see with and *I* as in myself," Luke said.

"Exactly, Luke. But there are homophones that are spelled differently based on their part of speech. Here it is...an article on Tricky Homophones," he said before reading it aloud.

Tricky Homophones

Homophones are words that share similar pronunciation but are spelled differently with different meanings. Some of the trickier homophones are related words that require a unique spelling based on their part of speech.

For example, *accept* and *except*. *Accept* is a verb meaning consent to receive. I accept your nomination for class president.

Except is most often a preposition meaning not including.
I will buy everything you have except for the orange socks.

A list of a few other tricky homophones, their meanings, and parts of speech follows.

advice	information	noun
advise	give counsel	verb
affect	make a difference / emotion	verb / noun
effect	change / cause	noun / verb
ate	consumed	verb
eight	number	adjective
bare	empty	adjective
bear	large mammal	noun
blue	color	adjective
blew	gusted	verb
bored	uninterested / form a hole	adjective / verb
board	piece of wood	noun
brake	device to slow or stop / slow or stop	noun / verb
break	shatter or destroy	verb
buy	purchase / a purchase	verb / noun
by	indicating / go past	preposition / adverb
counsel	guide / advice; lawyers	verb / noun
council	group of advisors	noun
do	perform	verb / helping verb
dew	tiny drops of water	noun
here	at this place	adverb
hear	perceive with the ear	verb
know	be aware; familiar with	verb
no	zero / not at all	adjective / adverb
lose	no longer have; unable to find	verb
loose	not firm or tight / set free	adjective / verb
made	formed	verb
maid	housecleaner	noun
our	belonging to us	possessive pronoun
hour	sixty minutes	noun
passed	leave behind	verb

past	time before	noun / adjective
peak	top	noun
peek	look quickly	verb
plain	undecorated; easy	adjective
plane	aircraft; flat surface	noun
their	belonging to them	possessive pronoun
there	at a place	adverb
they're	they are	contraction
then	at that time; therefore	adverb
than	used in comparisons	conjunction / preposition
threw	sent with force	verb
through	moving through something / toward completion	preposition / adverb
to	identifying location or noun	preposition
two	number	adjective
too	also; excessive	adverb
weather	state of atmosphere / wear away	noun / verb
whether	expressing doubt or alternatives	conjunction
your	belonging to 'you'	possessive pronoun
you're	you are	contraction

The children looked over their father's shoulder to see the unique spellings. "I'm going to have a hard time remembering all of these," Luke said.

"But you remembered the ad for the WOE act, right?" the queen asked, suddenly excited.

"Yes. I remembered the picture of the word looking upset," Luke said.

"What if we made pictures to help people remember how to spell tricky homophones?" the queen asked. "Maybe they wouldn't be so quick to support the WOE bill."

"That's a superb idea, my queen!" the king said. "We could show them to members of Parliament."

"Father, what does it take to be a lobbyist?" Kirk asked.

"Lobbyists meet with members of Parliament and share information to change their opinion," the king explained.

"Do you think we could be lobbyists too?" Kirk asked.

The king stroked his beard thoughtfully before speaking. "I don't see why not! But you're going to need help. We will have to lobby

Parliament and create some ads of our own. And you'll need to send out a mission to the guardians," the king said.

"Already working on it," Ellen said smiling. "We'll call it Tricky Homophones."

What does *apprised* mean?

What are two sets of tricky homophones?

Why did Luke know about the WOE bill?

Chapter 16

The king finished his breakfast in a hurry. He was eager to meet his friend Ernie, who was going with him to the galaxy's biggest golf tournament. All the professional players would be there. The two had gotten tickets months in advance.

The king couldn't wait to see his favorite professional players up close. He hoped that Ernie would be on his best behavior. Ernie had a tendency to tell the same stories over and over. He also frequently forgot his wallet, forcing the king to pay his way for whatever they were doing. But Ernie could also be a lot of fun.

When Ernie arrived at the castle, he was in good spirits. He suggested they take the space copter to the tournament. "I don't have clearance for that, Ernie," the king told him.

"Okay, how about the space porter then?" Ernie asked **beseechingly**.

★ ★ ★ ★ ★ ★ ★ ★ ★ ★
beseechingly – *pleadingly*
★ ★ ★ ★ ★ ★ ★ ★ ★ ★

"I reserve that for urgent matters. You know that," the king reminded him.

"It's urgent that we get to the tournament. Do you know how crowded it will be? We'll be waiting for hours if we take the space tram. What's the point of being king if you can't enjoy the perks?"

The king thought for a moment, stroking his beard. "Come on!" Ernie pleaded with him.

"Okay," the king relented. "Just this once," he said, grinning.

The two used the space porter in the castle and arrived at the golf tournament in seconds. "Amazing!" Ernie exclaimed. "I don't know why you don't travel this way all the time."

The king ignored Ernie's comment and began looking for the entrance. "There it is!" he said, pointing to the long line to their left.

"Ugh," Ernie groaned. "We'll be out here all day waiting. And it's already hot," he complained, wiping his brow. "Can't we cut in line because you're the king?"

The king was obviously **torn** as he estimated their wait time. "I can't, Ernie. It wouldn't be fair. These people arrived before we did."

★ ★ ★ ★ ★ ★ ★ ★ ★
torn – *undecided*
mobility – *movement*
★ ★ ★ ★ ★ ★ ★ ★ ★

Ernie was obviously annoyed as they took their place at the end of the line. He folded his arms across his chest and sighed.

A tournament staff member drove a few attendees with **mobility** challenges toward the front of the line in a golf cart. He stopped when he saw the king. "Your Majesty, what are you doing back here?" he asked. Before the king could explain, he encouraged him to hop on the golf cart.

"Could my friend come too?" the king asked.

"Absolutely!" the staff member said.

When the two men were on the golf cart, the king smiled at Ernie. Ernie grinned back. He was just glad they weren't stuck in that line.

The king was so excited about being able to watch the players from close up that he didn't mind that Ernie hadn't brought his wallet.

The two decided to watch all the players on one green. Ernie pushed to the front of the crowd by announcing that the king was coming through. The king wasn't happy about Ernie's pushiness, but they did have a great view as people moved aside.

Ernie and the king enjoyed watching play on the green, but they were tired at the end of the day. They had been standing for hours, and the sun was intense.

As the two were leaving, a reporter spotted the king and asked for a quick interview. Though he was worn out, the king agreed.

"What did you think of getting to see the top players in the galaxy up close?" the reporter asked.

"It was good," the king said.

Good? the reporter thought. *That's a strange response.* "How about seeing Lionel Forest sink that long putt?" the reporter asked.

"That was just fine," the king said.

The reporter looked at him quizzically. "What would you like to say to Lionel?" he asked the king.

"You had a positive performance," the king answered.

The reporter hesitated. "All right. What did you think of the tournament itself? And what did you think of the food?"

"Spectacular!" the king answered.

The reporter wanted to determine whether he meant the tournament or the food. But he decided he needed to end the interview. He thanked the king for his time.

"You really must be tired," Ernie said as they walked away. "Drink some more water."

The king didn't answer but took a swig of water. When they were away from the crowd, he used his communicator to transport them back to the castle.

When they arrived, the king reminded Ernie that he owed him for the shirt he'd bought him at the tournament. "I think I paid for everything last time we golfed. So we're even," Ernie said, grinning.

The king was too fatigued to argue and waved goodbye.

That evening the family watched the news coverage of the golf tournament together. "There you are, Father!" Ellen squealed when he appeared on the screen.

"The king didn't seem overly excited about today's tournament," the news anchor said. The video of his *good*, *nice*, and *positive* responses rolled. Attention shifted back to the news anchor. "He did seem excited about the food, however," he said, chuckling. The clip of the king calling the food spectacular rolled.

The king's face reddened. "Did you really not like the tournament, dear?" the queen asked with concern.

"I said it was good!" he said sharply.

The family grew quiet until Luke asked, "Was the food really spectacular? Wish I would have gone."

The king announced he was going to bed. "It's been a long day." The family murmured their understanding until he left the room.

"He seems overwrought," Kirk said.

"What does that mean?" Ellen asked.

"It means he seems concerned," Kirk answered.

"He seems fine to me," Luke replied.

"He seems superb," the queen added.

"The way father responded to that interview seems strange," Kirk said thoughtfully.

"It was unusual," Ellen agreed.

"It was outlandish!" Luke exclaimed.

"Bizarre even," the queen added.

"You know what, we're using strange vocabulary," Kirk said.

"Yeah. I don't even know what *outlandish* means," Luke agreed.

"Screen," Kirk ordered, "give me a status report on planet Vocabulary."

"Your Highness, I have nothing noteworthy to report from planet Vocabulary," Screen reported.

"Please check again," Kirk requested.

"I have checked for events and news stories and do not see anything out of the ordinary," Screen responded.

"I know it's a vocabulary problem," Kirk said. "Let's check the guidebook," he suggested. The three English children went to the castle library. There they began searching the glossary of *The Guidebook to Grammar Galaxy* for vocabulary topics.

"It's like we're not saying what we mean," Ellen thought aloud.

"Right, Ellen. We need an entry on word meanings. Meaning, meaning," Kirk murmured as he searched the glossary. "Wait! What's this? Shades of meaning." He turned to the page indicated in the glossary and began reading to his brother and sister.

Shades of Meaning

Words can be synonyms (similar) yet still be different in intensity.

For example, *good* and *spectacular* are synonyms, but the word *spectacular* has a higher intensity than good. *Mad* and *furious* are synonyms with *furious* having a higher intensity than mad.

To communicate well, it is important to choose the synonym with the correct shade of meaning. Rather than choosing any synonym from a thesaurus, read definitions and example sentences. Make sure the synonym and your intended meaning match.

"That was practical," Ellen said.

"It was crucial information," Luke added.

"We're still having a problem with shades of meaning, and we don't know why. We are going to have to go to planet Vocabulary and investigate."

"Now?" Ellen asked, obviously surprised.

"No, it's too late. We'll leave first thing tomorrow," Kirk said.

"That will be pleasant," Luke said. His brother and sister sighed.

The next day the three guardians asked their father's permission to go to planet Vocabulary. They explained Screen's lack of explanation for their vocabulary problem. And they shared what they'd found in the guidebook. The king readily agreed and praised his children for being leaders.

Kirk directed the space porter to take them to Synonym City. He suspected the root of the problem could be found there.

Once they arrived, they walked the streets and noted nothing unusual. "Let's visit some of the synonyms," Ellen suggested. The three walked into one of the apartment buildings where the words lived. They saw furniture movers working on every floor. The three looked at one another knowingly.

Kirk suggested they speak with the building manager. When they found her in her office, Kirk said, "I see many furniture movers working here today."

"Yes!" she said breathlessly. "We wanted to abide by the terms of the Fairness Act as soon as possible.

"Fairness Act? What's that?" Kirk asked.

"It's all explained in this letter," the manager said, handing it to him.

Kirk quickly scanned the letter. "This letter says that synonyms cannot be housed by intensity. Regardless of meaning, words have to be randomly assigned a floor to live on. It says buildings that don't comply with the Fairness Act will be shut down. It's signed by the director of the Good to Great Galaxy Commission.

"Ma'am," Kirk said, "we don't know anything about this Act or Commission. I'm sorry to say that we're going to have to put these words back in the apartments they were in."

"You're kidding me," the manager said, exasperated. "I don't even know which apartments the words were in. If you read the letter, you know that we aren't to have any evidence of assigning apartments by meaning. So I destroyed the records."

"Oh no!" Ellen exclaimed.

"It's going to be a lot of work to figure out where the words should be. But I know just the people for the job," Luke said cheerfully.

"Right, Luke! We have to create a mission for the guardians. Then we'll get the words back where they belong," Ellen agreed.

The manager asked the movers to stop working. Then the three English kids used Kirk's communicator to craft a Shades of Meaning mission.

What does *beseechingly* mean?

What are shades of meaning?

Why was the English family using the wrong words to communicate?

Chapter 17

The king was practicing his putting out on the castle's putting green. He was determined to sink a relatively long putt when his butler distracted him. "Your Highness!" he called. The king's shot rolled right of the hole.

"Blast it!" the king grumbled. "What is it that's more important than golf?" he asked the butler.

"My apologies, Sire. It's just that there is a situation on planet Spelling," he explained.

"Again? What is wrong with that planet lately? I need to appoint a new governor."

"Yes, well, the existing governor is waiting to have a video conference with you," the butler said.

"Did you tell him I was busy?" the king asked, frowning.

"I told him you weren't immediately available, but he insisted he talk with you. He says it is urgent."

The king sighed and put his putter in his golf bag. "Will you have this returned to the castle?" he asked, pointing to his bag. "It's obvious I won't be working on my game today."

The butler agreed and the king walked reluctantly back to the castle. He mopped his forehead with his golf towel as he went. He considered getting a cold drink and a snack before taking the call but thought better of it.

Another servant met him at the door and said that the governor was waiting on screen for him in his office.

Once the king arrived in his office and took the call, he said, "I'm afraid you caught me at an **inopportune** time, Governor. I'm sure it's urgent or you wouldn't have insisted on talking," the king said to reprimand him.

★ ★ ★ ★ ★ ★ ★ ★ ★ ★

inopportune – *inconvenient*
impending – *coming*
expedition – *trip*

★ ★ ★ ★ ★ ★ ★ ★ ★ ★

"Yes, Your Highness. It is indeed urgent. We had a ship from Math Galaxy land here on planet Spelling," he said breathlessly.

"A Math Galaxy ship? I wasn't informed of an **impending** visit," the king said.

"The ship isn't here with visitors," the governor said ominously. "They're here to stay."

"Who's there to stay?" the king asked, suddenly concerned.

"The ship was loaded with numerals who want to settle here. They arrived with no papers of any kind. As soon as they were all on our soil, the ship left."

"Thank you for telling me. I'm going to contact the king of Math Galaxy and find out why his numerals made an unauthorized stop," the king said. He ended the call with the governor abruptly and asked Screen to connect him with the king of Math Galaxy.

When the king of Math Galaxy appeared on the screen, the king described what he had learned about the numerals landing on planet Spelling. "I'm sorry to say I have no knowledge of this **expedition**. I didn't approve it," the Math king said.

"I think I know who arranged it," the king of Grammar Galaxy said. "I'll set up a return flight for them immediately."

"I'm afraid that won't work," the Math king said sternly. "Numerals who leave without an approved operator lose their citizenship. They'll have to complete a new application to live here."

"You must be joking!" the king said.

"I'm afraid I'm not," the Math king said. "And we're months behind in processing citizen applications. If I were you, I'd find a way to help the numerals live peacefully in your galaxy."

The king was fuming. He thought of several things to say that he knew he shouldn't. "I hope you will exercise better control of your citizens in the future," the king said.

The Math king's face reddened. He started to speak but seemed to think better of it. "I'm confident that you can find a way to coexist with the numerals. But if not, they can return when their citizenship applications are processed. Good day," he said, ending the call.

The king was furious. He knew he needed to calm down and the best way to do that was to talk with his wife. He found her in the kitchen talking with Cook. "May I have a few minutes, dear?" he asked her.

The queen noticed his demeanor and raised her eyebrows in Cook's direction. She moved to the dining room with her husband and asked what was going on. The king explained everything he had been told. "Could the Math king be working with the Gremlin now?" the king worried aloud.

"I don't think so, dear. Math Galaxy has its own problems. Their king wouldn't have time to interfere in our galaxy," the queen said.

"I suppose you're right," the king said. "The Gremlin could have arranged this on his own. So, what are we going to do with hundreds of numerals on planet Spelling? It's a planet for letters," the king said.

"It's not just for letters, Your Highness, if you don't mind me saying so," Cook said, joining them in the dining room. "Look here," she said, pointing at her cookbook. "My recipes have numbers in them. I'm to add 1 ½ cups of chocolate chips and bake the cookies at 350 degrees."

"Is this the recipe for your Out-of-This-World Chocolate Chip Cookies?" the king asked.

"The very same," Cook said proudly.

"Of course there are numbers in the recipe. I don't know what I was thinking," the king said.

"There are plenty of numbers in the book on investing that I'm reading now as well," Cook said.

"You're reading about investing?" the king asked.

Cook laughed at his surprise. "Certainly! I want to grow my money and not just save it," she said.

"You've given me an idea, Cook. Two ideas actually," the king said. "First, if you'll make me a batch of those amazing cookies, I'll add a bonus to your salary that you can invest. Deal?" Cook eagerly agreed. "My second idea is that we can get those extra numerals working on planet Spelling."

"How?" the queen asked.

"I'll explain when the kids meet us in the library," the king said.

Later, when the children were gathered in the library, the king explained what had happened with the numerals and the Math king.

"What are we going to do with numbers on planet Spelling?" Luke asked.

"I'm glad you asked," the king said. He opened *The Guidebook to Grammar Galaxy* and began reading an entry called "Writing with Numbers."

Writing with Numbers

Numbers should sometimes be spelled out and at other times should be left as numerals in writing.

WHEN TO SPELL OUT NUMBERS

- **Numbers one to nine should be spelled out.** The girl grabbed *five* pencils.
- **Numbers at the beginning of a sentence should be spelled out or the sentence rearranged.** *Sixteen* students enrolled in the class. The school enrolled *16* students.
- **When numbers appear next to each other in the text, one number should be spelled out.** He ordered *75 nine*-inch nails.
- **In dialogue or quotes, numbers should generally be spelled out.** "I'm going to need *fifty* cupcakes."
- **When spelling out numbers, two-word numbers under 100 should be hyphenated.** "I counted out one hundred twenty-five buttons."

WHEN TO USE NUMERALS
- Use numerals for dates and numbers larger than nine. By *1865*, more than *600,000* soldiers had died in the Civil War.
- Use numerals for decimals. (Add a zero for decimals less than one.) The chance of being struck by lightning in your lifetime is *0.0003* or 1 in 3000.
- Use numerals to stay consistent in describing something in a sentence, even if it breaks another rule. She counted *5* of *20* pens that worked.
- Use numerals in science writing or directions. Add *4* ounces of vinegar to *2 ½* tablespoons of baking soda.

WHEN TO USE BOTH SPELLING AND NUMERALS
- When writing about millions and billions, mix numerals and words. Over *140 million* books have been published to date.
- When choosing whether to spell a number or use a numeral in writing, use a style guide. Or ask the teacher or publication you're writing for.

After the king had finished reading, Luke said, "I have a question." When his family encouraged him to ask it, he said, "If the chance of being hit by lightning in my lifetime is only one in three thousand, why do I have to come inside every time there's a storm?"

The rest of the family groaned. "Luke, let's focus on the problem at hand," the king said. "If we can get more people writing with numerals, we can use the new numbers that arrived on planet Sentence."

"Yes! We would just have to make sure we aren't overusing them, right, Father?" Ellen asked.

"Correct!" the king said proudly.

"We have a mission, don't we?" Kirk asked, smiling.

The king returned his smile. Then he guided his wife out of the library and toward the kitchen, where he was hoping to find his favorite cookies.

The three English children worked on a mission called Writing with Numbers.

What does *impending* mean?

Should you use a numeral or spell out a number at the beginning of a sentence?

Do you think the king will allow the numerals on planet Spelling to stay? Why or why not?

Unit III: Adventures in Grammar

Chapter 18

The king received a call on Saturday afternoon. He had just finished his workout and was hoping to take a nap. He reluctantly took the call on his communicator.

"Yes," he said **tersely**.

"So sorry to bother you, Your Highness. But I thought you should know that here on planet Sentence we have quite a few words gathering for what appears to be a tailgating party. I've called in extra Grammar Patrol to keep it **contained**."

The king was relieved when he realized that the captain wasn't reporting a crisis. "I see. Well, we do have an important Galaxy Cup match later today. I understand why they would want to tailgate, don't you?" the king asked.

"Certainly, Your Highness," he answered quickly.

"And there's no law against tailgating that I know of," the king said.

"No, Your Majesty."

"Let them have fun," the king concluded, hoping to get off the call quickly.

"Yes, Sire," the captain said.

"If there are any problems, let me know. Otherwise, carry on." The king ended the call and went to take a shower and a nap.

The king awoke after a short time and found Luke right outside his bedchamber door. "I'm glad you're awake!" Luke exclaimed. "Want to watch the Galaxy Cup match with me?"

The king chuckled. "I certainly do! In fact, I think we should have some tailgating food while we watch."

"What's tailgating?" Luke asked. "Does it have good food?"

The king laughed. "Tailgating is when people have a party in the lot surrounding a sports stadium. Gasoline-powered trucks had a tailgate or hinged piece that opened to load or unload cargo. Many years ago, people would drive their vehicles to parking lots for matches. They would open their tailgates to unload tables and chairs and even barbecue grills. They would sit next to their vehicle to eat, socialize, and even occasionally watch the match on TV."

"Wow! But we don't have a tailgate and we're not at the stadium," Luke pointed out.

"We don't and we aren't. But we can have Cook make us up some burgers and hot dogs to eat while we watch."

"Yes!" Luke said, pumping his fist enthusiastically. He led the way to the kitchen to place their food order.

Later, with tailgating food in hand, Luke and the king sat in the media room to watch the Galaxy Cup. "They're—, they're—, the anthem of each team is being...do you hear the music?" the king asked Luke.

"Yes, they will be—, they will be—, it will start soon," he answered.

The king nodded, focused on the screen.

When the players took the field, the crowd shouted its approval. The announcers began describing the play. "Oscar, of the..., of the.... team, is..., is...excuse me, I seem to have a bit of a catch in my throat."

"This play is certainly exciting enough to leave you speechless," a second announcer joked. "Team Vocabulary has the ball. Louis is..., is...I have a catch in my throat too. I think the air is dry here in the booth," he said.

The king wasn't pleased. "They're..., they're..., what on English? How can we all have a catch in our throats at the same time?" he thought aloud. "Luke, is your throat okay?"

"Yes! My throat is just fine. I'm just...just...uh-oh."

"Not during the Galaxy Cup!" the king groaned. He was about to ask Screen to research the problem when he remembered the call he'd gotten from the captain of Grammar Patrol. "It's the tail—, the tail—. Screen, get me a view of the Galaxy Cup party on Planet Sentence," he ordered.

Screen immediately responded with an **aerial** view of a large gathering of words.

★ ★ ★ ★ ★ ★ ★ ★ ★ ★
aerial – *midair*
★ ★ ★ ★ ★ ★ ★ ★ ★ ★

"There are thousands of them!" Luke exclaimed. "They're soccer fans too!"

"Screen, zoom in, please, so I can see which words are gathered," the king said. Soon the words *penalized, playing, passed, shooting,* and *punted* came into view. As Screen panned the crowd of words, the king groaned. "Participles."

"They're participants?" Luke asked.

"No, participles. But they are in fact partici—, I won't be able to say it. I said there was no problem with these words tail—, with them...let's just say the party is a big problem! We have to break it up immediately. Go find Kirk and Ellen and meet me in the library," the king said.

Luke did as he asked. When everyone was in the library, the king read aloud the article on participles from *The Guidebook to Grammar Galaxy*.

Participles

Participles are verb forms that can be used as part of a multi-word verb, as adjectives, or as nouns. Participles are present or past in form. Participles used as adjectives or nouns are also known as verbals.

<u>Participles as Verbs (Actions)</u>

Present participles always end in *-ing*.

I have been *listening* to the music for hours.

have – helping verb; been – past participle; listening – present participle

Past participles for regular verbs end in -ed.

I had *listened* to the music for hours.

had – helping verb; listened – past participle

Past participles for irregular verbs vary.

I have *bought* you some new music.

have – helping verb; bought – past participle, irregular verb

<u>Participles as Adjectives (Descriptors)</u>

Participles as adjectives may be present or past.

I have a new *swimming* suit. – present

I ran into the *closed* door. – past

<u>Participles as Nouns/Gerunds (Things)</u>

Gerunds always end in -ing.

Swimming is my favorite sport.

I don't like *lying*.

"What is—, what is—, what is the problem with participles?" Ellen asked.

"They are at a party on planet Sentence." The king asked Screen to produce a video of the party to show her. "You'll have to ask the participles to leave," he said.

"Is that safe?" Ellen asked nervously.

"Good point. I'll make sure you have backup from Grammar Patrol," the king reassured her.

"Then we can't watch the Grammar Cup?" Luke complained.

"It won't be fun to watch unless you break up that party," the king explained.

"We'll need to send out a mission if we want to work quickly," Kirk added.

"Indeed!" his father answered.

The three English children worked on a mission called Participles. They then used the space porter to arrive at the tailgating party as quickly as possible.

What does *contained* mean?

What is a gerund?

What are some examples of participles the sports announcers couldn't say?

Chapter 19

The King joined his family in the media room after taking a phone call. He looked **morose**.

"What is it, dear?" the queen asked.

"I just received a phone call from the Galactic Sports Federation. We have been invited to participate in the Grammar Dash," the king said.

"Grammar Dash?" Kirk said. "What's that?"

"I know what it is!" Luke said. "It's an obstacle course race."

"You children have always loved obstacle courses," the queen said in a **reverie**. Are you all going to participate?" the queen asked.

"There are conditions to our participation," the king said tentatively. When the family urged him to continue, the king explained. "We all have to participate. If we do, a donor is prepared to give $1 million toward our library budget."

"That's a lot!" Luke exclaimed. "I'll do it. I think it will be fun."

"It sounds like a worthy cause," Kirk added.

"If the boys are doing it, I'm doing it," Ellen said.

105

"What kinds of obstacles are they?" the queen asked nervously.

"That's the issue, dear," the king said. "This is a mudder."

"What do you mean, a mudder?" the queen asked.

Luke's eyes grew wide. "It's a race through—. It's obstacles in the—

"It's mud!" Luke blurted out.

"Mud? Oh, my stars! I've never been one to play in the—, in the—," the queen stuttered.

"I know, my dear," the king said, rescuing her. "We don't have to participate, the king said.

"It's for charity," Luke pleaded.

The queen glanced down at her dress, picturing it covered in mud.

"Clothing can be washed," Ellen said, guessing her thoughts. "That's what you've always told me when I didn't want to get dirty."

The rest of the family held their breath, waiting for the queen's answer. "All right," the queen said hesitantly. Her husband and children applauded.

"This is going to be fun," Ellen said, hugging her mother's neck.

"It's not going to be on TV, is it?" the queen asked.

"Oh, probably not," the king answered. "I don't think they'll be interested. We're not professional athletes," he chuckled. The rest of the family laughed.

Several weeks later, the royal family stood in a crowd of hundreds of people at the starting line for the Grammar Dash. The queen wore a suit specifically designed for the event. She frowned at the cameras positioned all around them, which she was sure were focused on her.

The king joked with other participants and seemed to be looking forward to the race.

Everyone gave attention to the race director when he used a bullhorn. "I'm going to tell you the obstacles you face ahead," he said. "Knowing them and completing them are two different things, however." Many in the crowd chuckled. "First on the agenda is the Down to—, Down to—. It's our first obstacle where you will get close to the—, close to the—. Let's just say you're going to be muddy," he teased.

"What did he say the obstacle was?" the queen asked the king.

The king was straining to hear the director himself. "I don't know. Let's just listen," the king said.

"The next obstacle you'll **encounter** is Pain Time," the director said. "You'll be hanging from—, hanging from—; you'll be up high, let's say that," the director said, grinning.

★ ★ ★ ★ ★ ★ ★ ★ ★ ★
encounter – *meet*
★ ★ ★ ★ ★ ★ ★ ★ ★ ★

"What did he say will be hanging from?" the queen asked.

"I don't know. Just listen!" the king said harshly.

The queen's feelings were hurt. But she felt better when she realized that the king was probably anxious about the race. That was especially true given all the cameras pointed his way.

The director continued. "The next obstacle you will face is the Summit Plummets," he said. You will climb up a—, up a—; you will climb up and then you will climb down," he said, enjoying his listener's eagerness.

"What are we climbing up?" the queen asked—mostly to herself this time.

Kirk came close to his parents. "Are you hearing the directions for the obstacles so far?" Kirk asked

"Yes, yes, I hear him just fine, Kirk," the king said, waving him away.

"Father I don't mean *hear* him exactly. He isn't giving thorough directions. I don't know how I can compete if I don't know what we're doing," Kirk explained.

"We'll understand as we go," the king said.

The director continued speaking on his bullhorn. "If you don't pass through the—, if you don't pass through—, you will be disqualified."

"If you don't pass through the what?" Ellen asked her father.

"I don't know," the king admitted. He glanced at Kirk who raised his eyebrows. "Something's wrong," the king said. Kirk nodded.

"Are we going to compete in the—, in the—?" the queen began.

"I suspect we won't be able to unless we deal with the Gremlin's latest shenanigans," the king said. We're going to have to use the space porter to get back to the castle immediately."

When the family arrived in the castle, the king led them to the library. "Screen," the king ordered once there, "give me any news you have of prepositions on planet Sentence."

"Prepositions? Do you think there's an outbreak of prepositions? I know my prepositions. I should be immune, right?" Ellen asked fearfully.

"I know them too!" Luke added.

"I don't believe this is a prepositions problem exactly," the king said. Soon Screen displayed a news story. Words were being led away by people carrying signs that read "Words are words, not objects."

"What does that mean?" Kirk asked. "Words are not objects."

"Just as I suspected," the king said. "Kirk, get out *The Guidebook to Grammar Galaxy* and read the article on objects of—, objects of—. Look up objects and I'll point to the article we need," the king said. Soon Kirk found the article on objects of prepositions and began reading.

Objects of Prepositions

The noun or pronoun at the end of a prepositional phrase is the object of the preposition. The object of the preposition answers the question *What?* after the preposition.

He is afraid of the dark.

Of is the preposition. *Afraid of what?* Dark. *Dark* is the object of the preposition (OP).

Modifiers or descriptors of the object of the preposition are separate parts of speech.

I love to sleep in a big, comfy bed.

In is the preposition. *Sleep in what?* Bed. *Bed* is the OP. The word *a* is an article adjective, while *big* and *comfy* are adjectives describing *bed*.

"If we don't get the prepositions back, no one is going to get over those—, through those—. You know what I mean," Ellen said.

"I do know what you mean," the king said. "I don't know where those objects have been taken. But I know you three need to get to planet Sentence to find them as soon as possible," the king said.

The three English children nodded. "We're going to ask the guardians for help too, right?" Luke asked.

"Indeed," the king said, smiling at his youngest son.

"Do you think you can work quickly enough that we can still participate in the Grammar Dash?" the queen asked nervously.

"I hope so," the king said. "In fact, the two of us need to return to the race. I have an idea for stalling it." The queen followed her husband reluctantly, while the three English children began working on a mission called Objects of Prepositions.

What does *encounter* mean?

What is an object of a preposition?

Why couldn't the director describe the obstacles?

Chapter 20

At Saturday morning's breakfast, the queen announced that she and Ellen were going shopping.

"For what?" the king asked. "Not clothes, I hope. You already have all the clothes you need."

"Father, you don't understand. We always need clothes," Ellen said, grinning.

The king snorted as though he didn't agree. "Just don't spend a lot," he warned. The queen and Ellen nodded sweetly. "Kirk and I are going to be at his robotics competition today. I know it's a long day, but it will be fun. Would you like to join us, Luke?"

"No," Luke said. "Me don't want to go."

Before the king could chastise him, the queen asked Luke if he wanted to go shopping with them instead.

"No, me don't," Luke said.

"Luke, I understand not wanting to go, but don't talk that way," the queen corrected him.

"What way?" Luke asked. "Me don't want to go shopping or to the robotics tournament. Me want to stay here," he said, pouting.

The queen caught the king's eye as if to say he should decide what to do. "What will you do if you stay home?" the king asked.

"Me will take Comet for a walk. Me can play catch with the butler. Him said he would play with me. Me can find things to do."

"Luke, are you feeling all right?" the king asked.

"Yes, why?" Luke asked. "Me just want to stay home today. You can ask the butler and Cook to watch me. Please?" Luke pleaded.

The king frowned and then sighed. "I supposed it would be all right this once," he said.

"Thank you, Father," Luke said, excusing himself. "Me going to take Comet for a walk right now." Comet **trailed** the boy out of the room

★ ★ ★ ★ ★ ★ ★ ★ ★ ★

trailed – *followed*

★ ★ ★ ★ ★ ★ ★ ★ ★ ★

eagerly.

The queen asked Kirk and Ellen to go get ready to leave. When they were gone, the queen whispered to the king, "I think I know what's wrong with Luke."

"You do? I'm glad because he was worrying me," the king said.

"Yes. I think he is jealous of the time we spend with Kirk and Ellen. He wants to have the attention he got as a baby. So he is using baby talk."

"Hm. I just know I don't like it at all," the king said.

"I know. I'll spend some special time with him this evening." Ellen had come back to the dining room as she finished speaking, so the queen dropped the subject.

After the queen and her daughter had spent a few hours shopping, the queen suggested they have lunch. Ellen loved having lunch out with her mother. The two agreed on a restaurant and were seated at a secluded table. The waitress came and took the queen's order.

When it was Ellen's turn to order, she said, "Me thinks me will have the sandwich special."

The queen was startled to hear her daughter use baby talk like Luke had. *Could she have heard me say I wanted to spend extra time with Luke?* she wondered. She hoped the baby talk wouldn't continue.

But when the waitress asked if the two wanted dessert, Ellen spoke for both of them. "Us both want the hot fudge sundae."

"No!" the queen interjected without thinking. "I mean yes. We'll have a hot fudge sundae, but we'll split it," she said, smiling apologetically. "I hope that's okay," she asked her daughter. Ellen nodded happily. *Hm,* the queen thought, *maybe she does need special attention.*

At the robotics competition, the king was proud as he watched Kirk work with his team. But later as he and Kirk watched other teams compete, the king was worried. Kirk was speaking strangely. It was almost like the baby talk Luke had been using. But why? He hadn't been **neglecting** to spend time with him.

★ ★ ★ ★ ★ ★ ★ ★ ★
neglecting – *failing*
★ ★ ★ ★ ★ ★ ★ ★ ★

When the family reunited later for dinner, the queen greeted her husband with a kiss. "Me missed you today. Thank you for being so generous," she said.

The king smiled warmly but then thought a moment."What did you say?" he asked.

"Me said me missed you. You're having hearing trouble hearing again, aren't you?" the queen said teasingly.

"No, me isn't," the king said. He gasped when he realized what he'd said. "Us are all using baby talk."

The queen realized it was true. "What do you think is wrong?" she asked.

"Me don't know, but me is going to find out," the king said. "Screen, give me a status report on planet Sentence."

"Your Highness, there are no reports of **unrest** on the planet," Screen said.

★ ★ ★ ★ ★ ★ ★ ★ ★ ★

unrest – *conflict*

★ ★ ★ ★ ★ ★ ★ ★ ★ ★

"All right. Is anything else of interest happening there?"

"The only thing I'm finding is a documentary team has begun filming there."

"Documentary? Who are they filming?" the king asked.

"The subject of the documentary is pronouns, Your Majesty."

"Subjective pronouns. Of course!" the king said. "Thank you, Screen. Children, is it all right if we delay dinner? Us has a problem," the king said.

The kids agreed to follow their father to the castle library. Once there, the king read them an entry in *The Guidebook to Grammar Galaxy*. It was on subjective versus objective pronouns.

Subjective vs. Objective Pronouns

Pronouns take the place of other nouns and can be subjective or objective.
Subjective pronouns take the place of subject nouns. They often appear at the beginning of sentences. Subjective pronouns do the action of a sentence or are what is being described. Subjective pronouns are *I, we, he, she, it, they,* and *you.*
  We left right on time.
  I am so cold.
Objective pronouns take the place of nouns acting as the direct object, indirect object, or object of the preposition. Objective pronouns include *me, us, her, him, them, you,* and *it.*

The coach invited *him* to playoffs.
The teacher gave *her* an award.
This spot is just for *us.*
Objective pronouns cannot be used as the subject of a sentence. *You* and *it* may be used as both subjects and objects.
Her was the first girl in line. – incorrect
She was the first girl in line. – correct
You hit *it* too hard. – correct
To remember which pronoun to use with compound subjects or objects (more than one), use only one pronoun. If it sounds wrong, try switching from objective to subjective or vice versa. Use the pronoun *I* or *me* last in compound subjects and objects.
Me and Caleb are going to the store. – check compound subject
Me is going to the store. – incorrect
Caleb and *I* are going to the store. – correct
I'm getting popcorn for *she* and *I*. – check the compound OPs
I'm getting popcorn for *she*. – one pronoun, incorrect
I'm getting popcorn for *I*. – one pronoun, incorrect
I'm getting popcorn for *her* and *me*. – correct

"Me still don't understand why we're talking this way," Luke said.

"Me suspects it's because all of the pronouns are the subject of a documentary. All pronouns are subjects now," the king said.

"So what can us do?" Kirk asked.

"Instead of being the subject of the documentary, us can have some of them called the object of the documentary. By official order," the king said. "Me will need you to take the paperwork to planet Sentence."

"And us will need the guardians to help," Luke said. "As soon as us eats," he said, grinning.

The three English children later completed a mission they called Subjective vs. Objective Pronouns.

What does *unrest* mean?

What is a pronoun you shouldn't use as the subject of a sentence?

Why did Luke sound like he was using baby talk

Chapter 21

The royal family took their seats at the All Stars Spaceball game. They had been looking forward to it for weeks.

The king balanced a hot dog, nachos, and a drink on his lap. The queen **donned** her sunglasses as their seats were in the sun. Kirk began reading the program. Ellen scraped at her frozen lemonade with a spoon and Luke watched the players.

★ ★ ★ ★ ★ ★ ★ ★ ★

donned – *put on*

★ ★ ★ ★ ★ ★ ★ ★ ★

"This is going to be great," Luke said, wriggling in his seat. He pulled his ball cap lower to shade his eyes. "Who's on first, Kirk?" he asked.

Kirk looked up from the program. "Who?" he asked.

"Right, who's on first?" Luke asked again.

Kirk looked at the program and said "Who" again.

"Don't you know how to read this program?" Luke said, gruffly pulling it from Kirk's hands.

The queen sternly reminded Luke of his manners and told him to return the program.

"But he won't tell me who's playing," Luke complained.

"What," Kirk said, searching the program that he had back in his possession.

"You heard me, Kirk. You just don't want to tell me what's in the program," Luke said, frowning.

"What *is* in the program. I told you," Kirk said, his voice rising.

"What is in the program? How would I know? You're the one looking at it, and you won't give it to me," Luke said, fuming.

★ ★ ★ ★ ★ ★ ★ ★ ★ ★

"What are you two **bickering** about?" the queen asked.

bickering – *arguing*

★ ★ ★ ★ ★ ★ ★ ★ ★ ★

"Who's on first?" the king asked as the fielding players took their positions. He hadn't been listening to the boys' argument.

"Yes," Kirk answered. "Who's on first."

"You don't know?" the king asked. "I thought who was playing what would be in the program."

"Who and what are in the program," Kirk said.

"That's what I'm asking you," the king said impatiently.

"I said Who's on first. What is on second," Kirk said.

The king shaded his eyes with his hand and looked out to second base. "I don't see anything on second base," the king said.

"What's on second base," Kirk said.

"That's what I'm asking you," the king said.

Kirk smacked the program on his lap in frustration. The queen observed this, worried that her son was in a rebellious phase. "Why are you upset about who's on second?" she asked.

"Who's on first, What's on second, and Whom is on third," Kirk said, exasperated.

"Whom is on third?" the king asked.

"Yes," Kirk said.

Luke tried to pull the program from Kirk's hands again. "Whose program is it?" Kirk asked.

"Mine!" Luke exclaimed.

"No, mine!" the king said, taking the program triumphantly. "Now who's on first?" he asked himself aloud as he scanned it. "Who is on first," he said, glancing at the program.

"Yes, who is on first, dear?" the queen asked.

"Who is on first," the king said.

"Why are you **mimicking** me," the queen asked. "Who is on first?"

"I told you Who is on first," the king said slowly.

"No, you didn't. Tell me who is on first," the queen said.

The king glared at his wife. "Why are you being so difficult?" he asked her.

Ellen slurped some melted lemonade from her cup. "What is this about who's on first?" she asked innocently. The rest of the family glared at her. "What?" she asked again.

Kirk sighed. "What's on second," he said.

Ellen shaded her eyes and looked out to second base. I don't see anything but a player. What's his name?"

"Right," Kirk said.

The announcer's voice interrupted their discussion. "Which is up to bat for the Vocabulary League," he said.

"Which player?" the king asked.

"Yes, Which," Kirk said.

"Who?" Luke asked.

"No, Who's on first," Kirk said.

The king used his binoculars to look at the player in the batting box. "Which is up to bat."

"I don't know! I can't see." Luke held out his hand for the binoculars and the king passed them to him.

"That's Which! And finally, I know Who is on first," Luke exclaimed.

"Right!" the king and Kirk said in unison.

"What is going on?" the queen asked. "I don't understand spaceball at all," she said, squinting at the field.

"What isn't doing anything right now," Luke said. "But he will if Which gets a hit."

"Which?" the queen asked.

"Right," Luke said.

"I don't know much about spaceball either, Mother, but I do know something is wrong," Ellen said.

"The game's just getting started," Luke said.

"I know, but we've been arguing about who, what, and which ever since we sat down. Haven't you noticed?" Ellen said.

117

"What?" the king said. The stadium was loud. The queen repeated what Ellen had said. The king took a bite of hot dog and thought as he chewed. The queen noticed his worried expression.

"What is it?" she asked.

"What, who, whom, which. They aren't ballplayers' names. What was I thinking? Children, I am so sorry, but I'm afraid I'm going to need your help right away. Something is wrong on planet Sentence, but I don't know what."

"You don't know if What is part of the problem?" Kirk asked.

"No, I don't know what is the problem with these pronouns. Listen, you three need to use the space porter to go home immediately. Look up interrogative pronouns in *The Guidebook to Grammar Galaxy*. Then have Screen help you research what is going on," the king said urgently.

"So you want us to research what specifically?" Kirk asked.

"Yes, what specifically is going on," the king said.

"But not who?" Kirk asked.

"Yes, who too," the king said, getting irritated again.

Luke looked disappointed that he had to leave the game and Ellen noticed.

"Father, would it be all right if Kirk and I worked on this by ourselves? Luke could stay and watch the game then," Ellen suggested.

Luke stood to hug his sister. "Who's your favorite sister?" she asked. Then she quickly said, "Don't answer that. Kirk, let's go and figure out what is happening," Kirk nodded and followed her out of the stadium.

When the two English children arrived in the castle, they ran to the library. They found the article on interrogative pronouns in the guidebook. Ellen read it aloud.

Interrogative Pronouns

The five interrogative pronouns are used to ask questions. They are *who*, *whom*, *what*, and *which*. The possessive pronoun *whose* may also be used as an interrogative pronoun. The answer to the question is the antecedent (noun replaced by the interrogative pronoun). But it may be unknown.

Who took my pen?
Whose shoe is this?
What day is it?

Who, whom, and *whose* are used to ask questions about people. What and which are used to ask questions about people or things.

Who is used when the answer is the subject of the sentence. *Whom* is used when the answer is a direct object, indirect object, or the object of a preposition. Note that *whom* generally isn't used in conversation or informal writing.

Whom was hit by the ball?

The suffix *-ever* may be added to interrogative pronouns to show surprise or confusion.

Whatever did you think you were doing?

"What do we do now?" Ellen asked. "What am I saying? Let's ask Screen what's happening on planet Sentence."

After some searching, Screen's only news from the planet was about the pronoun documentary they already knew was in progress.

"That's strange," Ellen said. "What could be causing the confusion with interrogative pronouns then?" she asked.

"I think I know," Kirk said. "What do you do if you're making a documentary?" he asked.

"What?"

"Yes, what?"

"Shoot videos," Ellen answered tentatively.

"Right. Of what?" Kirk asked.

"Well, in this case, pronouns," Ellen said.

"Right. And you're asking the subject of your documentary questions," Kirk said.

"What's your point?"

"My point is they're asking the interrogative pronouns questions. The only answer they can give is *what, who, whom, which,* and *whose*," Kirk said.

"I don't know," Ellen said.

119

"You don't know if that explains the problem we're having?" Kirk asked.

"I don't know what, who, whom, which, and whose."

Kirk sighed. "Okay, we're going to assume that the interviews are causing the problem. They may be interrogating these pronouns and the only answer they can give is what," Kirk said shrugging.

"I don't know," Ellen said.

"El, I'm going to ignore what you just said." When Ellen started to say what, Kirk put a finger to his lips. "Let's get to work. We'll need the guardians to help us identify interrogative pronouns. As Guardians of the Galaxy, we will tell the documentary filmmakers that interrogative pronouns cannot be interviewed. We'll need our fellow guardians' help to get them all excused."

Ellen nodded and picked up a pair of reading glasses lying on the desk. "Whose are these?" she asked.

Kirk took them from her. "Let's get an Interrogative Pronouns mission out to the guardians. When we get back from planet Sentence, I think all your questions will be answered."

What does *mimicking* mean?

What are two interrogative pronouns?

Why did Kirk think they were overusing interrogative pronouns?

Chapter 22

The king announced to his children that they would be leaving the next day for planet Sentence.

Kirk asked, "What's the crisis, Father?"

"That's just it," the king answered. "We need to be **proactive** and visit before there's a problem. I know the citizens of planet Sentence will appreciate seeing us."

★ ★ ★ ★ ★ ★ ★ ★ ★

proactive – *act before*
resolutely – *determinedly*

★ ★ ★ ★ ★ ★ ★ ★ ★

The kids thought that made sense. The king had his public relations person set up a time for him to address the citizens of the planet. The king asked his children to be prepared to say a few words as well.

"What are you going to say?" Luke later asked Kirk. "I don't know what to say."

"Father said it didn't have to be long," Kirk said.

"I know, but I still don't know what to say. What are you planning to say?"

"Luke, I don't want to tell you and have you copy me," Kirk said **resolutely**.

Luke groaned. "I'm going to go ask Mother what to say then."

Luke found his mother in her office and explained his uncertainty about what to say in his speech.

"Luke, what is the purpose of this visit to the planet?" the queen asked.

"Father said it's a good-will visit. He wants the citizens to know he cares about them."

"Okay, so how can you say something that communicates that?" she asked.

"I guess I could say I'm happy to be there because I rely on them," Luke said hesitantly. Then he seemed more enthusiastic. "I could say that they do a great job and I could thank them!"

"Yes, that's a lovely idea! I knew you could do it, Luke."

"Thanks, Mother."

The next day, the king and his three children stepped onto the outdoor platform where they would be speaking. Luke felt ready—excited even.

A large crowd of words had gathered to hear their king. Luke felt so proud of him as he was introduced. His father was an excellent speaker. "Good afternoon, fellow citizens of the galaxy. Together we have been able to defeat the Gremlin and keep this galaxy strong. But I have a warning for you: Never leave alphabet soup on the stove and then go out. It could spell disaster." The words in attendance expressed their appreciation for the king's joke.

But as the king continued his remarks, he was interrupted by noise to his left. A separate group of words had gathered and were loudly expressing disapproval. The king was distracted and stopped speaking. When he couldn't **discern** what the issue was, he struggled to continue. But the noise from the group increased. Soon everyone in the crowd was staring at the words and ignoring the king.

★ ★ ★ ★ ★ ★ ★ ★ ★ ★
discern – *determine*
★ ★ ★ ★ ★ ★ ★ ★ ★ ★

Suddenly, some men dressed in black appeared on stage. They grasped the royal family members firmly by the shoulders. "We have to get you out of here now!" one of them shouted. "Follow us!"

When the king resisted, the leader of the group said, "You're in danger! We can't delay!" The king then agreed to go with the men and urged his children to follow him.

The four of them were rushed to a black space copter that lifted off immediately. After they were safely in the air, the king shouted to the pilot, "What's the danger? What's going on?"

"Your Majesty, the demonstrators at your speech—we don't know what they're capable of. They may be violent. In fact, the Gremlin may have sent them specifically to harm you or the kids."

"Really? That's surprising because the Gremlin isn't known for violence," the king said.

"Enemies like the Gremlin always become more dangerous with time," the pilot shouted back.

The king nodded, thinking. "So what were those words demonstrating about? What is making them so unhappy?" he asked.

"Oh, a variety of things. You've done plenty to make them mad, right? We just didn't want to take any chances."

I've done plenty to make them mad? the king repeated to himself. He was surprised but willing to listen to the pilot, who obviously knew more about the situation than he did.

"Where are you taking us?" the king asked.

"We have a safe house on the planet designed for emergencies like this one," the pilot said proudly.

The king nodded, feeling very uneasy. He joined his children in looking at the scenery below the copter.

After the space copter landed, several men in black ushered the four royals into a dark room in the basement of a plain building. "How long will we need to stay here?" the king asked one of the men.

"Until we get the situation contained," he said gruffly.

"And what is the situation again?"

"We'll explain when we have finished our investigation."

"I see," the king said grimly.

"Do you have any food here?" Luke asked.

"We'll see if we can round something up," the man said, closing the door behind him.

"Father, I can't get a signal on my communicator. I think the building is designed to block communication," Kirk said.

"What? I don't like the feel of this at all," the king said, pacing. He walked over to try the door and was not surprised to find that it was locked. "We have to find a way out of here," he told the kids.

"And it won't be with the space porter. It won't work from inside this building," Kirk said, punching buttons on his communicator.

"Is there a bathroom in here?" Luke asked.

"Don't tell me you need one right now," Ellen said.

"I don't," Luke said defiantly. "If there's no bathroom, I think I can get us out of here." He pounded on the door. "Hey, guys! I have to use the restroom!" he called, smirking at Ellen.

They heard a man complain to his partner but he came and unlocked the door. "Okay, this way, but you'll need to make it quick. We don't want any of those demonstrators to hurt you," the man told Luke.

"Sure thing," Luke said cheerfully. The man pointed to the door of the restroom and Luke went in. But Luke kept the restroom door opened a crack so he could see what the guards were doing. They weren't looking his way. He quickly spotted the staircase they had come down.

Quietly, Luke tiptoed to the staircase and began climbing the stairs. Just when he thought the men would turn to see him, his sister Ellen pounded on their locked door. "Could we have some water?" she asked. "We're very thirsty."

The men's attention turned to the room he'd left, giving Luke time to scramble up the stairs. He checked for additional guards. He spotted one near the front door and was deflated. He moved rapidly to search for a rear door and was delighted to find one that was unguarded. He slipped outside and put out an emergency signal with his communicator. When a dispatcher responded, Luke asked her to send Grammar Patrol to his location immediately. He asked her to contact the queen about their situation as well.

He disconnected the call and slipped back into the building. He started tiptoeing down the stairs when he was stopped by the two men he had seen earlier.

"What are you doing? You're going to get yourself killed!" one of them chastised him.

"I heard Ellen asking for water and I was looking for some upstairs. Didn't find any though," Luke said, shrugging.

The men eyed him suspiciously. "We got you some water already," one growled.

"Oh, thanks!" Luke said cheerfully as he reentered the room with his family.

After the door was locked behind him, Luke whispered to his family that help was on the way.

"Luke, you lied to those men, and you know how I feel about lying," the king said.

"I know, but—," Luke started to defend himself until the king interrupted him.

"But in this situation, you did it to protect your family," the king said, hugging Luke gratefully. Luke smiled and felt proud of himself.

After what seemed like hours, the family could hear space copters overhead. They could hear several people talking, footsteps on the stairs, and then the door to their room was unlocked.

"Your Majesty! We are so thankful you are all right," the Captain of Grammar Patrol said.

"We're thankful you're here. Can you tell me what is going on?" the king asked.

"There was a group of demonstrators at your event today. Your private security team here believed they were a threat."

"They're not my private security team. I thought they were working with you!" the king said angrily.

"They're not?" The captain looked confused. "That can only mean one thing," he said soberly. He used his communicator and called for his men to detain the private security guards.

After a few moments, one of the officers messaged back. "Sorry, Captain. We missed them. They're gone."

The captain punched his fist into his palm. "I'm sorry, Your Majesty."

"That's all right," the king said. "I'm just glad we're okay. But I do want to know more about these demonstrators."

"Certainly," the captain said. He removed his communicator and showed the king pictures of them. The king laughed. "What's so funny?" the captain asked.

"Those aren't demonstrators. They're demonstrative pronouns. *This*, *that*, *these*, and *those* point out specific things. When used alone as in '*This* is my daughter,'" he said, pointing to Ellen, "they're pronouns. When used before nouns as in '*This* boy is my son,' they're adjectives. They weren't protesting anything and they certainly aren't dangerous."

"That makes sense," the captain said.

"You used a demonstrative pronoun!" Luke told the captain. "Now I'll use a demonstrative adjective. This stomach," he said pointing to his belly, "is growling. Let's get something to eat."

The group laughed. "Father, I agree with Luke that we should eat. But when we get home, I think we should send out a mission on demonstrative pronouns to the guardians," Kirk said. "I wouldn't want to go through this again."

"That is a great idea!" the king said, chuckling.

What does *proactive* mean?

What are the four demonstrative pronouns?

Who do you think the private security team was working for?

Chapter 23

The royal family had finished dinner. The king announced it was the perfect evening to play some tennis together.

Everyone agreed to change and meet on the tennis court. Once there, the king and Kirk faced Ellen, Luke, and the queen. The king hit practice balls to the three of them. Kirk would try to hit any **errant** balls back over the net.

The queen complained of being rusty.

★ ★ ★ ★ ★ ★ ★ ★ ★ ★

errant – *wayward*

commended – *praised*

★ ★ ★ ★ ★ ★ ★ ★ ★ ★

"You should be out here practicing more often, dear," the king suggested.

"I'm practicing now," she said, defending herself.

"Luke, follow through," the king said as Luke's ball sailed over the baseline.

"I like spaceball better," he grumbled as he got behind Ellen to wait for another ball.

"Beautiful forehand, Ellen," the king **commended** her.

"More topspin," he told the queen. She grimaced.

"I don't know how to hit with topspin," she complained.

"Kirk, show her how to hit a ball with topspin," the king said.

Kirk took a ball from the basket, dropped it in front of him, and hit the ball over the net. He hit himself in the back with his racket at the end of his swing. "Ow!" he exclaimed.

"Kirk, that follow-through was a bit too much," the king said, chuckling. Kirk nodded, slightly embarrassed. "It was a good shot with plenty of topspin though," the king said. "Okay, dear. Now let's see you hit the ball with topspin," he told his wife. "You want to brush up on the back of the ball. That will keep the ball in the court," he said, demonstrating with his racket.

"Okay," the queen said **tremulously**. She tried to hit the ball as instructed and was pleased at first contact. She followed through by bringing her arm up and over her shoulder. But then she shrieked in pain as she hit her back with her racket. "Ow!" she cried.

★ ★ ★ ★ ★ ★ ★ ★ ★ ★

tremulously – *tremblingly*

★ ★ ★ ★ ★ ★ ★ ★ ★ ★

"All right," the king said. "Follow-through is good, but stop hitting yourselves. Are you okay, dear?" he asked, remembering to be sympathetic.

The queen nodded, but she seemed upset.

"Okay, Luke. Let's see your topspin," the king said, ready to hit a ball to his youngest son.

Luke was in the ready position, determined to impress his father. He began his stroke as his father had demonstrated. But like his mother and brother, he hit himself in the back at the end of the swing. He bit his lip to keep from crying out in pain.

The king looked disappointed in him. "Ellen," he said. "Let's see if you can hit the ball without hitting yourself," he said, trying to be funny. The queen and the boys didn't laugh.

Ellen readied herself for the ball and concentrated. She would not hit herself with the racket, she told herself. Yet after hitting the ball, her arm swept across her body and *smack*! She felt the racket painfully connect with her back. She couldn't hold back the tears. Not only did it hurt, but she knew she hadn't hit the ball right.

The king was clearly irritated with them. "Tennis is not a contact sport," he said. "I don't understand how you are getting hurt. Follow through, but don't bring your racket so far over your shoulder. Okay?"

His family members were slow to agree. "Dear, hit this ball and show the kids how easy it is," the king told the queen. When she seemed reluctant, he said, "Don't worry about topspin. Just hit the ball." He smiled encouragingly.

The queen felt more confident in simply hitting the ball. She took her position and struck the ball forcefully. But once again, she finished her swing by hitting herself in the back.

This time, Ellen rushed to comfort her. She hoped it would stop her father from doing more tennis drills that evening. The king joined them on the other side of the net to make sure his wife was not seriously injured.

"Don't say anything!" the queen warned as he walked toward her.

The king stepped back in surprise. "I wasn't going to. I just don't know how you keep hitting yourself," he said innocently.

"That's exactly what I didn't want you to say," the queen said angrily.

"I guess we have to stop playing for tonight," the king said, hoping his family would disagree. When they didn't, he asked them to gather the balls.

After returning to the castle, the king tried to lighten the mood. "Why don't we watch a movie together?" he suggested. The queen and the kids grudgingly agreed. "How about a comedy?" He was relieved when he got a positive response.

In the media room, the king asked Screen to give them some family-friendly options. After choosing one, the family settled down to watch. Perhaps it was the frustration they experienced on the tennis court that led them to laugh a lot at the movie.

Kirk slapped his thigh as he laughed. "Ow!" he said.

The king laughed. "You slapped yourself too hard? That's funny," he said.

"I guess I did," Kirk said, staring at his hands.

When a few minutes passed, Luke cried out in pain too.

"Did you just slap yourself when you were laughing?" the king asked him.

"Yes," Luke was embarrassed to admit.

"What is it with you hitting yourselves tonight?" the king asked, shaking his head. When he returned his attention to the movie, he heard a smack and then a gasp coming from the queen's direction.

The queen's eyes filled with tears. "Before you say anything," the queen said, "know that I did not try to hit myself. It just—it just happened!" she said.

Ellen smacked herself in the forehead.

"What is it, Ellen?" the king asked. "Did you remember something?"

"No," Ellen said tearfully. "I just hit my forehead and I wasn't trying to."

"You weren't trying to?" the king said. "This is worrisome," he said, standing and walking toward the Screen. "Screen, stop playing the movie. Search for causes of uncontrolled movements."

After a moment, Screen produced a list of diseases and conditions. The king quickly dismissed most of them. Then he gasped. "Food poisoning. What did you eat that I didn't eat?"

"Vegetables?" Ellen suggested.

"Yes! That could be it. I did not eat any of the vegetables tonight. And you all did?" the king asked.

The rest of the family nodded wearily.

"I'm going to have to inform Cook," the king said, exiting the room briskly.

When Cook learned that her vegetable dish had sickened the royal family, she hit the side of her head.

"Don't punish yourself, Cook," the king said kindly.

"I do feel bad, but I didn't mean to hit myself, Your Highness," Cook said, her eyes wide.

"Did you eat the vegetables?" the king asked.

Cook nodded, trembling.

"I'll have to call the doctor," the king said, smacking his fist into his other palm. The king bent over in pain. "I didn't mean to do that," he moaned. "And it hurt."

"But Your Highness, you didn't have the vegetables," Cook said.

"I know. I could kick myself for not realizing what this is," he said. His leg suddenly bent behind him, connecting painfully.

"Are you all right?" Cook asked, eyes wide.

"Yes," the king groaned. "But I have to put a stop to this or I won't be."

The king left the kitchen and found his family still sitting in the media room. He explained that the problem wasn't food poisoning at all. "Screen, is anything new happening with the documentary on pronouns?" he asked.

"Your Highness, pronouns are being given thorough physicals to make sure they aren't being overworked," Screen said.

"That's it," the king said, smacking himself in the forehead. "Ugh!" he exclaimed, rubbing the red mark he made there.

"What is it, Father?" Kirk asked.

"I'm going to have *The Guidebook to Grammar Galaxy* brought in and then I'll explain," the king said.

When a servant arrived with the guidebook, the king read them an article called Reflexive Pronouns.

Reflexive Pronouns

Reflexive pronouns are pronouns that end in *-self* or *-selves*. Reflexive pronouns include *myself, oneself, ourselves, yourself, yourselves, himself, herself, itself,* and *themselves*.

Reflexive is Latin for reflect. Reflexive pronouns are direct and indirect objects that reflect back to the subject.

I hit *myself* with a hammer. – direct object
I gave *myself* a haircut. – indirect object

Reflexive pronouns cannot serve as subjects. A common error is to include a reflexive pronoun in a compound subject. To detect the error, remove the other subject from the sentence.

Joe and myself are going fishing this weekend – incorrect
Myself is going fishing this weekend. – subject removed, incorrect
Joe and I are going fishing this weekend – correct

Another common error is to use a reflexive pronoun as an indirect object that does not match the subject.

You can give Jane and *myself* the money later. – incorrect
(*myself* doesn't match the subject *you*)
You can give Jane and me the money later. – correct

> You can give me the money later and I'll buy myself a treat. – correct
> (*myself* matches the second subject *I* in *I'll*)
>
> **Reflexive pronouns may also be used as intensive pronouns.** They intensify or emphasize the subject or antecedent to show that someone else did not do the action. Intensive pronouns may be removed from a sentence without changing the meaning.
>
> I made the pie crust *myself*.
> We *ourselves* moved the furniture.

Kirk slapped himself on the thighs in understanding. "That makes sense. But I myself don't see the connection between reflexive pronouns and the documentary," he said.

"I myself suspect that the physical exam pronouns are getting includes a reflex test," the king said. "The reflexive pronouns are the only pronouns with reflexes. When they respond, we're hitting ourselves," the king said, punching his fist into his palm again. He groaned.

"What can we ourselves do?" Luke asked.

"I myself should be able to get new physical exams stopped. The directors themselves need to have legal permission to do physicals. I bet they don't have it. But that won't help with the pronouns who are already getting physicals. I need you yourselves to identify the reflexive pronouns on planet Sentence. You'll tell them that they're needed in the king's service, so they'll be excused."

"But we can't do all that ourselves," Luke said. "We need the guardians."

The king agreed, and the royal English children created a mission called Reflexive Pronouns. When they were done, they left for planet Sentence.

What does *commended* mean?

What are three reflexive pronouns?

What was being done to the reflexive pronouns that was causing problems for the English family?

Chapter 24

"What are you doing, dear?" the king asked. His wife was on the floor of their bedchamber closet, tossing clothes into a pile.

"Minimizing," she said, continuing to focus on the clothes in front of her.

"Minimizing, eh? It looks like you're making a maximum mess," the king said, chuckling to himself.

The queen didn't seem to have heard him. She stood up, smiling and breathless. "I'm getting rid of so much stuff!"

"Wonderful! I think. Will you be buying new clothes to replace these?" he asked warily.

The queen laughed. "No, silly. Minimizing means that you eliminate what you don't need, and you don't buy *more* things you don't need."

"Then I'm all for that!" the king said, grinning.

"I'm sure you are," the queen said, laughing. "When I finish my side of the closet, I'm going to work on yours."

"Uh, you're joking, aren't you? I don't have too many clothes," the king objected.

"You don't have too many clothes?" the queen said, astonished. "Let's just see," she said, marching over to her husband's closet. She pushed on the closet door that was already ajar. "Look! I can't even close this door!"

"I wear all of those! And I get rid of things I don't wear."

"Really? When was the last time you **purged** something?"

★ ★ ★ ★ ★ ★ ★ ★ ★ ★

purged – removed

★ ★ ★ ★ ★ ★ ★ ★ ★

"Oh, not long ago..." the king said, trailing off.

The queen was moving his hangers and removed a suit triumphantly. "When was the last time you wore this?" Without waiting for an answer, she continued. "You had this made when we celebrated Kirk's birth. You haven't worn it since!"

"I'm sure I have," the king insisted.

"Really?" the queen asked, eyes narrowed, daring him to prove it.

"Well, maybe I haven't, but I might wear it again when Kirk graduates from high school."

"Sure you will," the queen said, laughing. "I think it needs to go."

"If I give this away, will you leave my closet alone?" he pleaded with her.

"Not likely," she said teasingly.

"Just work on your own closet for now. I'll go through my things later," he pleaded.

"Mm-hm," she murmured with no confidence as she returned to her own closet.

That evening at dinner, the queen chattered excitedly about her closet cleanup. "I am giving away so many clothes!"

Ellen nodded encouragingly. "It feels so good to **streamline** your closet," she agreed.

★ ★ ★ ★ ★ ★ ★ ★ ★
streamline – simplify
★ ★ ★ ★ ★ ★ ★ ★ ★

"Yes! I was so motivated by the book *Less Are More*," the queen said.

"What did you say?" the king asked, looking up from his plate.

"I'm so motivated by reading *Less Are More*."

"That can't be right," the king said.

"It is right," the queen said steadily.

"No, dear. I know you're motivated to remove clutter and that's great, but that can't be right. I promise you."

The queen reddened. "Let me explain it to you. I know you haven't read the book," she said, trying to calm herself. "Anything you don't use or need are too much."

"That's not right either," the king said, shaking his head.

"Hmph," the queen retorted. "I suppose each of us are entitled to our own opinion."

"No, we're not," the king said.

"What? Everybody have loved this book. Several of my dresses is in boxes to go to charity and I am not putting them back in my closet. You're just upset because anything that are dusty old rags in your closet are more important to you than my feelings!" She abruptly got up from the table and left the dining room.

"Well, then," Luke joked. "I wonder what's for dessert?"

Ellen chastised Luke and then questioned her father. "Why don't you want mother to give away clothes she doesn't wear? I don't understand."

"There aren't anything wrong with your mother giving away clothes," the king said. Then he gasped. "Oh no. I should have known."

"You should have known what?" Kirk asked.

"That your mother's grammar wouldn't **deteriorate** just because she was excited about minimalism."

★ ★ ★ ★ ★ ★ ★ ★ ★ ★
deteriorate – worsen
★ ★ ★ ★ ★ ★ ★ ★ ★ ★

"What do you mean?" Kirk asked.

"The title of the book she read can't be *Less Are More*. And saying that anything you don't use or need are too much is wrong too. Screen," the king barked, interrupting himself. "I need a status report from Noun Town."

"Yes, Your Majesty," Screen responded.

"What nouns do you think are messed up?" Luke asked.

"Pronouns, indefinite," the king answered.

"So you think the pronouns are messed up but not definitely?" Luke asked.

Screen interjected, "Your Majesty, the proof of citizenship requirement you made is being enforced."

"What proof of citizenship requirement?"

"Indefinite pronouns on planet Sentence are now required to show proof they are citizens. Officials are stamping their certificates to show their status."

"I didn't authorize this!" the king roared. "What is being stamped on their certificates? That has to be the source of the problem."

Screen searched for and found a video of an indefinite pronoun's certificate being stamped. The king asked Screen to zoom in on the stamp. After he read it, he said, "That explains it."

"Everything are making sense now?" Kirk asked.

The king sighed. "It will make sense after we visit the library." He led the three children to the library. When they arrived, he explained the problem. Indefinite pronouns were being incorrectly marked singular or plural. He said they would understand after he read the article on indefinite pronouns in *The Guidebook to Grammar Galaxy*.

Indefinite Pronouns

Indefinite pronouns are pronouns that do not refer to specific nouns. To have subject-verb agreement with indefinite pronouns, learn which pronouns are singular and which are plural.

Indefinite pronouns ending in -one, -body, and -thing are always singular and take a singular verb.

Someone is in my seat! (singular verb)

Everybody has a place at the table. (singular verb)

Everything is beautiful! (singular verb)

Other singular indefinite pronouns include *another, each, either, much, little, neither,* **and** *other*.

Either is fine. (singular verb)

Much has been said about the topic. (singular verb)

The indefinite pronouns *both, few, many, others,* **and** *several* **are always plural.**

Few are able to pass the test. (plural verb)

Several have told me about the park. (plural verb)

Other indefinite pronouns are singular or plural depending on how they are used. They include *all, any, more, most,* and *some*.

When used with a noun that can be counted, use a plural verb.

Some of the quarters are on the floor. (quarters can be counted; plural)

When used with a noun that cannot be counted, use a singular verb.

Some of the flour is on the floor. (flour can't be counted; singular)

When used to describe a noun (rather than standing alone), the words *any, each, few, some, many, much,* **and** *most* **are indefinite adjectives. Verb agreement is with the noun.**

Any player who breaks the rules will be eliminated. (singular verb)

Some kids prefer to work alone. (plural verb)

"I am definite that I won't remember all that," Luke joked when his father finished reading.

"Don't worry, Luke. We know the right verb to use with some indefinite pronouns from experience," the king said. "They'll just sound wrong if paired with the wrong verb."

"And some of these is going to take practice, right, Father?" Kirk asked.

"Uh, you're right about the practice. But you should have used the verb *are* there, Kirk," the king said, looking pained.

"Everyone need to know which verb to use with indefinite pronouns, right Father?" Luke asked.

"Everyone *needs* to know," the king said, emphasizing the right verb form. "That includes the officials on planet Sentence. I need you children to go there and have them change the incorrect stamps on the pronouns' paperwork. And I'll make sure the proof of citizenship requirement is dropped."

"And let me guess...someone are sending out a mission," Luke said.

"Is!" Kirk, Ellen, and the king replied in unison.

The English children worked together on a mission called Indefinite Pronouns before leaving for planet Sentence.

What does *deteriorate* mean?

What are two indefinite pronouns that are always singular?

Why is the English family using the wrong verbs with indefinite pronouns?

Chapter 25

The queen went to pick Ellen up from Cher's house. Ellen had been so excited about Cher's sleepover birthday party. The queen looked forward to hearing all about it.

When she arrived, the queen thanked Cher's mother for having her daughter over, and Ellen graciously thanked her host as well.

As the two royals rode home on the space tram, the queen quizzed Ellen about her night. Ellen's eyes welled up with tears.

"What's wrong?" the queen asked, suddenly concerned.

"Do you remember Amy?" Ellen asked.

"Amy...I think you have mentioned her before," the queen said.

"She is a friend of Cher's. I don't think she likes me," Ellen said sadly.

"How could anyone not like you?"

"Oh, Mother, you don't understand!" Ellen said more loudly than she intended.

"I do understand," the queen said. "I was a young girl once," she said smiling. "Why don't you tell me what happened?"

"When it was time to watch a movie," Ellen began.

"Yes, when it was time to watch a movie, what?" the queen asked.

"When it was time to watch a movie," Ellen said again.

"Ellen, you can tell me. I'm not going to be upset," the queen reassured her.

★ ★ ★ ★ ★ ★ ★ ★ ★ ★

exasperated – *frustrated*

★ ★ ★ ★ ★ ★ ★ ★ ★ ★

"I know, Mother!" Ellen said, **exasperated**.

"What happened when it was time to watch a movie?" the queen asked again.

"When it was time to watch a movie," Ellen said. She stopped and covered her eyes and cried.

The queen put her arm around Ellen and hugged her. "Ellen, I'm sorry you're so upset. I'm here to listen when you're ready to talk."

Ellen nodded and sniffled. "After the movie was over," Ellen said.

"Yes, yes," the queen urged her to continue.

Ellen sighed. "Because..." she said.

"Because of what?" the queen asked, beginning to get annoyed.

"You don't understand!" Ellen wailed.

"No, I don't," the queen said. She gave up trying to hide her irritation. The two rode home the rest of the way in silence.

The king greeted the two of them when they returned to the castle. Ellen barely acknowledged her father and went straight to her room. The king raised his eyebrows and looked to the queen for an explanation.

"I don't know what's wrong with her," the queen said. "She was upset when I picked her up, but she won't finish telling me what happened. It has something to do with Cher's friend Amy."

Luke had walked into the room as the queen mentioned Cher and Amy. "Girls are so dramatic," he said, smirking.

"They can be," the king said, grinning in response.

"I recall a time when you were having a physical **altercation** with Max," the queen said to reprove him.

Luke reddened a bit. "Well, that was his fault, not mine," Luke said defensively.

"Doesn't matter if you're a boy or a girl. Conflict is something we all deal with," the queen said. Luke nodded and said he was going to have a bowl of cereal.

"Haven't you already had breakfast, young man?" the queen asked.

"Yep, this is second breakfast," Luke said, laughing.

"I think I'll join you," the king said.

The queen decided she needed to try speaking with her daughter again. She knocked softly on Ellen's bedchamber door. Ellen told her to come in. She didn't look any happier than she had on the ride home.

"Ellen, are you ready to tell me what happened?" the queen asked.

"If Amy hadn't asked Cher to sit with her the whole time," Ellen said angrily.

"Yes, so Amy was demanding Cher's attention?"

Ellen nodded. "If she hadn't wanted to sit with her the whole time," Ellen said.

"If she hadn't asked Cher to sit with her the whole time, what?" the queen asked. She was encouraged that Ellen was telling her more about what happened.

"That's it," Ellen said. "If she hadn't wanted to sit with her the whole time. Don't you understand?" Ellen said, clearly **peeved**.

"I understand that Amy tried to sit with Cher a lot during the party, but that's all," the queen answered.

★ ★ ★ ★ ★ ★ ★ ★ ★ ★
altercation – *fight*
peeved – *annoyed*
★ ★ ★ ★ ★ ★ ★ ★ ★ ★

"This is pointless," Ellen said.

The queen gasped. "What do you mean *pointless*?" the queen asked.

"If you don't understand what I'm saying," Ellen said.

"I do understand what you're saying," the queen insisted. "But you're not telling me everything."

Ellen buried her face in her pillow and cried.

The queen sighed. "Ellen, I think you're tired. You girls probably stayed up much later than normal. I'm going to let you get some sleep

141

and then we can talk about it when you're rested. The queen closed the door to Ellen's bedchamber and went to find her husband.

She found him in the dining room reading the paper. "You know you're not supposed to read at the table," the queen said.

"Well, you weren't here, dear, so I thought it was okay." He smiled up at her but noticed her expression. "What's wrong with her?" he asked with a suddenly serious expression. He put the paper down.

"I don't know," the queen said. "I know that Amy was trying to keep Cher's attention, but other than that I don't know."

"She won't answer your questions?" the king asked.

"She answers my questions, but she doesn't give me all the details."

"That's what tween girls do, dear."

"I know," the queen said sadly. "I just didn't know it would be so painful," she said, beginning to weep. The queen excused herself to her bedchamber. The king shrugged and picked up his paper again.

Luke burst into the dining room, beaming. "Because it's Saturday," Luke said.

The king hesitated a moment, waiting for him to continue. When he didn't, he said, "Because it's Saturday, what?"

"Because it's Saturday," Luke said as a statement.

"Okay, Luke, you got me. You're not going to tell me what's so special about Saturday?" the king said.

"Well, Saturday is a day off. I like Saturdays," Luke said.

"That's right, but it sounded like you had something else to say."

"No," Luke said nonchalantly.

The king scratched his head. "All right then. Have a good day." He picked up his paper and began to read when Kirk joined them in the dining room.

"Although I discovered my computer had a virus," Kirk said.

"Yes?" the king asked. Luke waited to hear his answer too.

"Yes, what?" Kirk said.

"Although your computer had a virus, what?" the king asked.

"Father, I know computer viruses aren't interesting to you, so I'll leave it at that."

"I know enough to understand what a computer virus is!" he said more angrily than he intended.

"I'm sorry, Father. I did not mean to offend you. If you'd like me to tell you about the virus," Kirk said.

"If you'd like me to tell you about the computer virus, what?" the king asked, a little calmer.

"If you want me to tell you about the computer virus," Kirk said again.

Just then Screen interrupted their conversation. "Your Highness, I believe a matter on planet Sentence is worthy of your attention."

When the king asked Screen to continue, a reporter appeared, speaking. "There is an exciting development here on planet Sentence. Independence has been declared for all clauses. No longer will some clauses be dependent on other more powerful clauses. They're all free."

"Now that the clauses are free," Kirk said.

The king groaned. "Now I understand what is going wrong with this family," the king said.

"Until you explain what you mean," Luke said.

The king groaned again. "Unless we do something right away," the king said. The boys gave him confused looks. "Now I'm doing it," he said with disgust. "We have to get your mother and sister in here. Luke, go and get them. Kirk, go and get *The Guidebook to Grammar Galaxy* from the library and bring it to me."

The two boys did what they were told. When Ellen and the queen arrived, the king explained the breaking news story they had heard. "Before you say anything," the king said, holding up his hand.

The King read them the entry on dependent and independent clauses.

Dependent and Independent Clauses

A dependent clause (also called a subordinate clause) requires an independent clause to make sense. An independent clause can stand alone as a complete sentence.

After we had dinner (dependent clause)
we went to a movie (independent clause)

When a subordinating conjunction joins dependent and independent clauses, a complex sentence is formed. Dependent clauses with a subordinating conjunction at the beginning of a sentence are normally followed by a comma.

After we had dinner, we went to a movie. (complex sentence)

See the chart with common subordinating conjunctions below.

Common Subordinating Conjunctions		
after	in order (that)	when
although	now that	whenever
as	once	where
as soon as	since	wherever
because	so that	whether
before	than	while
even if	that	why
even though	though	
how	till	
if	unless	
in case	until	

"Although I understand what a dependent clause is," Ellen said. The rest of the family waited for her to finish her thought.

When she didn't, the queen said, "Even though this is helpful information."

"We have to put a stop to this immediately!" the king exclaimed. "I don't know how much longer I can take it."

"But how can we take the clauses' independence from them?" Kirk asked.

"That's simple," the king said. "Planet Sentence's Constitution does not allow sentence parts to declare their independence. I suspect the Gremlin is behind this."

"If we go to planet Sentence," Ellen said.

"How will you deal with dependent clauses?" the king said, finishing her sentence. When Ellen nodded, he continued. "You'll need the guardians' help. Every dependent clause needs to be shown a copy of the planet's Constitution. They have no legal right to independence."

The three children nodded and began work on a mission they called Dependent versus Independent clauses.

What does *altercation* mean?

What is a dependent clause?

Why weren't the English children finishing their thoughts?

Chapter 26

The king and queen were watching the news after the children had gone to bed. The news anchor said, "And we end tonight's broadcast with a feel-good story..."

The king and queen looked at one another in surprise. "That's a nice change," the king said. The queen nodded.

"We are doing a follow-up story on a beloved artist from the hit shows Contraction and Abbreviation Nation. Inky, who became famous for adding periods and apostrophes to words on planet Spelling, has opened up a new shop on planet Sentence."

A video began showing Inky adding a colon to a sentence. "I love adding this mark to sentences," she said while she worked. "It really makes a sentence stand out. And I've found that that's what sentences are looking for. If they're not ready for a colon, I add a semicolon. Here's an example," she said, opening a photo album for the reporter. "I love making sentences happy."

"Oh," the queen gushed. "That's beautiful." She dabbed a tissue to her eyes. "I wondered whatever happened to her. It's clear she is happy too."

"You don't see anything amiss here?" the king asked, clearly astonished.

"No, should I?" the queen asked.

The king squirmed in his seat. "Did a colon belong in the sentence she was working on?" he asked, raising his voice slightly.

The queen grew nervous, recognizing her husband's agitation.

"Uh, what was the sentence? I don't remember. I just thought it seemed happy to be getting a colon."

The king jumped up in exasperation. "We are going to have a huge problem because of what she is doing."

"Don't you think you're judging her too harshly? Maybe adding ink to sentences isn't what you're interested in, but she loves it. And she's clearly good at it," the queen lectured.

"I am NOT judging her," the king said.

"Yes, you are," the queen insisted.

"It's late and I don't want to go to bed angry. So I will save this discussion for tomorrow with the children," the king said.

"Is it really that important? Or is it one of those small matters we can just let go? We had style preferences that our parents didn't like. Remember? I don't see this as being any different."

"Dear, this isn't a matter of style."

"Our parents didn't think so either," the queen said.

"Okay. I'm going to say goodnight. We'll talk about it tomorrow," the king said, trying to **reign** in his emotions.

★ ★ ★ ★ ★ ★ ★ ★ ★ ★

reign – *control*

★ ★ ★ ★ ★ ★ ★ ★ ★ ★

"Okay," the queen said cheerfully. "I'm going to stay up for a while longer."

The king left the room, shaking his head. He hoped a good night's sleep would help him communicate better.

The next morning, the king threw his newspaper down in disgust.

"What is it now, dear?" the queen asked, sighing.

"I'll tell you what it is," he replied angrily. "Inky's work has made it into the paper."

"Oh, they wrote a story about her new project?" the queen asked, perking up.

"I wish that were the case. Instead, there are misplaced colons and semicolons all over the sports page!"

"That doesn't seem that serious. Sportswriters' grammar isn't perfect. You know that," the queen chided him.

"Don't you see that Inky's colons and semicolons are behind this?" He pointed out the many colons and semicolons in the article he'd been reading.

"Hm. I do see what you mean. There are quite a few."

"Yes, there are!" he roared.

"I don't understand why you're so angry though. Inky seems like such a sweet girl."

"I think the Gremlin put her up to this," the king said through gritted teeth.

"Are you trying to cut back on coffee again? I don't think that's a good idea for you," the queen said in a **supercilious** tone.

★ ★ ★ ★ ★ ★ ★ ★ ★ ★
supercilious – *arrogant*
galore – *aplenty*
★ ★ ★ ★ ★ ★ ★ ★ ★ ★

The king told her he would cut back on coffee if he wanted to and left the dining room in a bad mood. The queen hoped he would work out his irritation at the gym.

She picked up her tablet and began reading an article on spring fashion in her *Woman's Universe* magazine. After reading a few paragraphs, a headache started. The queen increased the size of the font. She was getting older and knew she would need reading glasses before too long. But the font change didn't help.

She felt as though the sentences went on and on. *Why?* she wondered. She looked closely at them and gasped when she realized there were no periods in the article. Instead, there were colons and semicolons **galore**. *He was right*, she thought. *These colons and semicolons don't belong in most of these sentences.*

She thought about going to apologize to her husband but had another idea. When the children came to the dining room for breakfast, she explained the problem. "As soon as you're done eating, let's go learn about colons and semicolons from the guidebook. I'd like for you children to solve this problem before your father is through working out. We'll surprise him!"

Kirk, Luke, and Ellen loved the idea. In the castle library, Ellen found the article on colons and semicolons in *The Guidebook to Grammar Galaxy* and read it aloud.

Colons & Semicolons

A colon (:) is used to give more information. A semicolon (;) indicates a pause longer than a comma but shorter than a period.

Colons
Use a colon to share an item or list of items. Don't capitalize the items unless they are proper nouns.
Do the right thing: share.

I need the following from the store: French bread, eggs, and milk.

Use a colon between two independent clauses when the second explains the first. The first letter of the clause following the colon is normally capitalized. This is always true when several explanatory sentences or a quote follows.

I have a few rules for you: Clean up after yourself. Brush your teeth. And turn out the lights.
The captain gave this order: "All aboard!"

Capitalizing the first word in lists following a colon is optional unless the list items include complete sentences. In that case, use end marks. Be consistent with capitalization and end marks.

Please pack the following:
– pajamas
– toothbrush
– toothpaste

Things to say to a frustrated student:
– You've been working hard.
– Would you like some help?
– Would it help to take a break?

Semicolons
Use a semicolon to list items that contain commas.

We will be traveling to Lexington, Kentucky; Sioux Falls, South Dakota; and Billings, Montana.

Use a semicolon between two closely related sentences. Unlike sentences with colons, the second sentence is not capitalized.

We are a close family; we spend a lot of time together.

Don't use a semicolon after a dependent clause. Use a comma instead.

After we have dinner, we're going out for ice cream. – correct

Use a semicolon before the words *however*, *therefore*, and *for example* that introduce complete sentences. Follow them with a comma.

I'd like to go on the trip; however, I already have plans.

Use a semicolon before a conjunction connecting independent clauses when the first clause contains a comma.

I think you are smart, talented, and funny; and I'd love to hire you.

"Wow! That's a lot to remember!" Luke exclaimed.

"You'll get better with practice, and you can always look at the guidebook information again," the queen said.

"We need to write a mission for the guardians. And we need to get to planet Sentence right away," Kirk said.

"May I be the one to tell Inky that she can't add colons and semicolons to sentences just because it looks good? We have a connection," Ellen said warmly.

"Sure. But you have to help us correct the punctuation too. It's going to be a lot of work," Luke groaned.

The three of them worked on a Colons and Semicolons mission for the guardians. The queen hoped the mission would be complete in time to surprise the king.

What does *reign* mean?

You shouldn't use a semicolon after which kind of clause?

Why did the queen talk to the kids about the punctuation problem instead of the king?

Unit IV: Adventures in Composition & Speaking

Chapter 27

The king walked into the media room to find his three children engaged in a discussion.

"I want to go," Ellen said.

"Me too!" Luke added.

"It's very expensive," Kirk warned.

"Where do you want to go that's very expensive?" the king asked warily.

"To Movie Adventureland," Ellen answered. "You get to experience the movies like they're actually happening."

"Right. Like *Jumanji*," Luke said, "only for all kinds of movies."

"I knew they were building the resort, but it's finished now?" the king asked.

"Yes, and the ticket prices are **exorbitant**," Kirk said.

★ ★ ★ ★ ★ ★ ★ ★ ★ ★
exorbitant – *excessive*
ruffled – *messed*
★ ★ ★ ★ ★ ★ ★ ★ ★ ★

"Of course they are," the king said, frowning.

"So we can't go?" Ellen asked, already disappointed.

"Let me get some more information," the king said. "We'll see."

"'We'll see' from Father means no. From Mother it means yes," Luke joked.

The king smiled and **ruffled** Luke's hair. "'We'll see' means we'll see," he said.

That evening at dinner, the king explained that he had checked on the ticket prices for Movie Adventureland. He didn't think it was wise to spend so much to go.

"Aww," Ellen complained.

"There are other, more affordable theme parks, Ellen," her mother said to stop her complaint.

"I really wanted to go," Luke said. "There is nothing else like it."

"I knew it was expensive, but I was also hoping we could go too," Kirk admitted.

"You could save money to pay for tickets," the queen suggested.

"Even if I saved money from my birthday, got paid to walk dogs, and sold lemonade, it would take me forever to have enough," Luke complained.

The queen looked pleadingly at the king to reconsider. The king frowned and shook his head. As he looked at his children's disappointed faces, he had an idea.

"There is no guarantee this would work, but you could offer to write a review of the resort in exchange for free admission," the king said.

Ellen's eyes brightened. "We could do that!" she exclaimed happily.

"I'd gladly write something if I could go for free. I want to do the Jurassic Park attraction," Luke said, jumping up and pretending to run from a dinosaur.

"Hold on there, young man. Come sit down. You would have to write a high-quality review for them that would get people to buy tickets," the king said.

"Would we send them the review for their website?" Kirk asked.

"I don't see the resort being willing to give you free admission for that. I hadn't thought of it before, but what if you three started your own website? Then you could offer to write a review there and help them attract visitors?" the king said.

"I can build a website easily!" Kirk said. "I'll have our programmer help me."

"What will it be called?" Ellen asked. "How about *Ellen English and Her Brothers*?"

"That's a terrible name!" Luke said. "How about *Luke and Friends*?" he suggested.

The king interrupted before Kirk could make a suggestion. "A website isn't about you; it's about your readers. Who are the readers you are hoping to attract?"

"Other kids?" Ellen suggested. When the king nodded, she continued. "*Grammar Galaxy Kids*?"

"I love it," the queen said, smiling at her daughter.

"I guess that works. I like *Luke and Friends* better though," Luke said, smirking.

"Kirk, get busy working on the *Grammar Galaxy Kids* website. Ellen, you and Luke need to work on a letter for the Movie Adventureland resort. Explain your proposal. We'll wait to see if they agree to give you free admission. Even if they don't agree, you'll have learned something. You could make the same proposal to other resorts," the king said.

The English children were beaming as they talked about their proposal.

The next day, Kirk told the king he had already made progress on the website. The king told him that was good news because the resort may check out the website before responding to their proposal.

Later the king walked by the desk where the family put outgoing mail. He noticed a letter addressed to the Movie Adventureland Resort. It wasn't written to the attention of a particular person or department. He picked it up and held it up to the light. He was surprised to see Ellen's handwriting and the lines of notebook paper. He had to open it and see what his children had written.

Dear Movie Adventureland Resort,

How are you? We are doing well.

We saw that you opened your resort, and it looks

amazing. We really want to see the Jumanji and
Jurassic Park attractions. However, your ticket prices
are way too high and our father won't let us buy them.

So we have an idea. Will you let us come to the
resort for free if we write a review for you? We would
put the review on our new website. Please give us your
answer right away. We're excited!

Your friends,
Kirk, Luke, and Ellen English

The king sighed after reading the letter. He was thankful he had found it before it had gone out with the mail.

He went to find his children. When he did, he asked them to follow him to the castle library. He removed *The Guidebook to Grammar Galaxy* from its shelf and asked Ellen to read the article on business letters.

★ ★ ★ ★ ★ ★ ★ ★ ★ ★
impression – *reaction*
★ ★ ★ ★ ★ ★ ★ ★ ★ ★

155

Business Letters

Business letters are often written to create a professional **impression** and/or to persuade. The audience for a business letter is typically someone you don't know. Follow a specific format when writing a business letter.

Business letters should be typed on plain or letterhead paper. Letterhead paper already has your name or your company name and address printed on it. When using plain paper, put this information at the top of the letter.

Insert a line space and add today's date.

Then address the individual you want to read your letter. This should be a specific person. Do some research or call the business to determine who is in charge of the department you are writing to. Start the salutation with *Dear Mr.* or *Ms. Last Name* and end with a colon (:). When you don't have a name, you will have to write *To whom it may concern:*.

Add a line space after the salutation.

Then begin and continue your letter with no idents. Paragraphs are separated by line spaces. This is called block format. Your letter should have one-inch margins. You can set these in the word processing program you are using.

Be sure to provide all the information the person needs to understand who you are and what you want. Be polite and give your recipient reason to respond positively to your request. This is the most important part of a business letter.

Add a line space and then the closing followed by a comma. An appropriate closing for a business letter is *Sincerely* or *Cordially*.

Add two line spaces where you will put your written signature after printing the letter.

Then add your full name followed by your title (if any).

Finally, add contact information, such as your phone number, if it is not included in your letterhead.

Proofread your letter twice and ask someone else to proofread it for you too. See the sample business letter that follows.

GRAMMAR GALAXY
PROOFREADING

111-222-3333
EXCELLENCE.GG

January 10, 3000

Dear Ms. Wilson:

I am writing to inquire whether you are in need of proofreading services. As you know, proofreading is important to make a good impression with any written work.

I have years of experience in proofreading, and I have many satisfied clients. I would be happy to send you references at your request.

My rates are below industry standard, making my services affordable. But I also offer quick turnaround.

Please contact me to discuss your proofreading project. I look forward to hearing from you.

Sincerely,

Susie Guardian

Susie Guardian, Founder and CEO
GGProofreading@gmail.com

"Uh-oh," Ellen said. "I missed some of those things."

"Yes. I'm glad I found the letter before it was mailed out. I know you can write a better letter that is more likely to get a positive response," the king said.

"Did you give them our website name?" Kirk asked. Ellen shook her head. "You need to add it because it is looking great," Kirk said.

"I have an idea," Luke interjected. "We didn't know how to write a business letter, right? I bet the other guardians don't know how to write them either."

"So we send them a business letter mission?" Ellen guessed.

"Yes, but even better, we ask them to write a business letter to the resort too. The guardians could ask the resort to agree to our request because they want to read our review," he said.

"That's a great idea, Luke!" Kirk said. "The resort will know we have a bunch of readers, even though our website is new."

The English children worked together to write a new business letter to Movie Adventureland. Then they created a mission called Business Letters that they sent to the guardians.

What does *impression* mean?

What is one thing Ellen and Luke did wrong in writing their business letter?

What was Luke's plan to get the resort to agree to give them free tickets?

Chapter 28

When the children awoke, they were surprised to see their mother and father running around frantically.

"What's going on?" Kirk asked.

"The reporter from *Best Homes and Gardens* is going to be here any minute. She asked if she could come today because she had a cancellation," the queen said, gasping for breath.

"Why did you say yes if you weren't ready?" Luke asked.

"That would make us look like we aren't ready for a photo shoot all the time!" the queen exclaimed as though the answer were obvious.

"But we're not ready all the time, right?" Luke persisted.

Ellen shushed him. "How can we help?" she asked.

"Bless you!" the queen said, pausing to hug her. She asked the kids to put newspapers and magazines out of sight.

"Now hold on with those," the king interjected as the kids obeyed their mother. "I'll take them. I'm still reading them."

The queen sighed. "Just please put them somewhere else," she said, trying not to be irritated with her husband.

The king told Ellen that her mother was a little out of control in a low voice.

"I heard that!" the queen called.

Cook entered the room quickly with Comet barking at her heels. "Your Highness, I have tea ready to be served and I asked the gardener to make sure everything is **pristine**."

★ ★ ★ ★ ★ ★ ★ ★ ★ ★
pristine – *perfect*
★ ★ ★ ★ ★ ★ ★ ★ ★ ★

"Cook, you're a lifesaver, truly. Thank you!" the queen said. Cook blushed.

"I'm going to go help the gardener," the king said.

"Comet and I will come too," Luke said, calling the dog.

When the king and Luke had left, the queen said, "Now we can get his mess put away!" Cook chuckled.

The reporter arrived with a photographer. Both were very complimentary of the castle as they were invited in.

"I've never been before, and it's a lovely castle," the reporter said.

"Oh, thank you," the queen said **demurely**.

★ ★ ★ ★ ★ ★ ★ ★ ★ ★
demurely – *modestly*
protocol – *etiquette*
★ ★ ★ ★ ★ ★ ★ ★ ★ ★

"We'll be doing a story on the royal gardens, but I think we should come back to feature the castle, don't you?" she asked the photographer. He nodded. "It's my first story for the magazine and I'm hoping to impress the editor," the reporter admitted.

"I'm sure you'll do a fine job," the queen said reassuringly. "I'll take you to the gardens via the back patio. The king is already there waiting to meet you."

The reporter gasped when she stepped onto the back patio. "Gorgeous!" she exclaimed. "I want to get lots of shots we can use for the front cover."

The front cover! the queen thought gleefully. She knew the king would be thrilled. He was very proud of his gardens.

The king spotted the visitors and began walking toward them. He asked Luke and Comet to stay where they were. Not everyone was comfortable around dogs.

"Your Majesty, it's an honor to meet you," the reporter said, curtsying. The photographer agreed and bowed awkwardly, uncertain of **protocol**.

"The honor is all mine," the king said graciously. "I look forward to sharing the royal gardens with you and your readers." He gestured for the two to follow him.

"The grand design of the royal gardens has been in place for generations. But each new monarch adds his unique style. I want to show you the touches I've added to make the gardens my own."

The reporter and photographer were enthusiastic in response. The king was enjoying himself very much. "Are either of you afraid of dogs?" he asked. When the two said they loved dogs, he led them to Luke and Comet. He introduced Luke, and the magazine staff introduced themselves to Comet with a thorough petting.

The group then took their time in the gardens—the king giving the history and details and the reporter and photographer recording it all. The tour ended with tea and crumpets on the patio and an invitation for the two to return to the castle.

Several months later, the butler brought a priority package to the queen. She opened it and removed several copies of *Best Homes and Gardens*, featuring their garden on the front cover. She squealed with delight. She turned to the article and was ecstatic when she saw the pictures. The garden looked even grander in print than it did in person. She couldn't wait to show the king.

She found him in his office. "Guess what I have?" she said in a singsong voice.

"A bill for new clothes," the king joked.

"No, and you're not funny," the queen teased back. "I have the *Best Homes and Gardens* article!"

"Oh, let me see it!" the king said eagerly. He held a copy of the magazine near his office window so he could see it clearly. "It's magnificent!" he said.

"I know," the queen said, nodding and nearly in tears.

"Let's see what they said," the king said, opening to the article.

"The rest of the photos are just as spectacular," the queen said.

The king began reading the article and his smile faded. He began reading aloud. "'The original design for the gardens was created generations ago,' the king told us. But it must be replanted every hundred years. In addition, each new king adds his own special touches. The king is especially proud of a fountain he has added to the center of the garden."

"That's all correct, isn't it?" the queen asked, worried by her husband's serious expression.

"Yes, it's correct. That's not the problem."

"Then what is? She didn't misquote you, did she?"

"Not that I've read so far."

"I think you're being overly picky again. It's not your best quality, dear."

The king's eyes flashed and a blood vessel in his temple bulged. He took a deep breath to control himself. "This is not a good article by any standard. Yes, the photos are lovely. Yes, she got the facts straight. But it's missing something critical."

The queen folded her arms across her chest. "Okay. I can see I can't change your mind. But I love the article and I'm going to tell my friends all about it!" she said defiantly. She left the room abruptly and the king read further.

He asked Screen to summon the children and to have the butler bring him *The Guidebook to Grammar Galaxy*. When they arrived, he showed them the magazine.

"Oh, it's exquisite!" Ellen enthused.

"Yes, the photos are gorgeous," the king admitted.

"You must be so happy," Ellen said.

"Congratulations, Father," Kirk added.

"Unfortunately, I'm not happy with the article. Your mother thinks I'm being too picky, but I feel strongly about this. I want to read you the article about descriptive writing from the guidebook."

Descriptive Writing

Descriptive writing uses words to describe subjects so that a picture is formed in a reader's mind. Word pictures are created with sensory words, analogies (similes and metaphors), or both.

<u>Sensory Words</u>

Sensory words are strong vocabulary words related to sight, sound, smell, taste, and touch. Before writing a descriptive first draft, make a list of sensory words that describe your subject. Sensory words that could describe cotton candy include:

– sight (turquoise, hot pink, whipped, airy, fluffy)

– sound (grinding motor of the machine, shrill call of the salesperson, pleading children's requests)

– smell (fruity, sweet)

– taste (sugary, tangy)

– touch (sticky, gritty, smooth cone)

<u>Analogies</u>

Before writing your descriptive first draft, consider what your subject is like, using a simile or metaphor.

The cotton candy was like a cloud in my hand. (simile)

The cotton candy was a truffula tree that I chopped down eagerly. (metaphor)

Organize Your Description

Once you have ideas for descriptive language ready, decide if you will organize your description chronologically (by time), by importance, or by location.

– Buying the cotton candy, eating it, and cleaning up after it (chronological)

– Being excited to eat the candy, only to discover it is too sweet (importance)

– Seeing the cotton candy in a machine outside a stadium and later eating it in the stands (location)

Refer to your sensory words and analogies as you write your description chronologically, by importance, or by location.

"May I see the *Best Homes and Gardens* article again?" Ellen asked. She began skimming it when the king handed it to her. "There is no descriptive writing in this article," she concluded.

"Exactly!" the king replied, pleased that his daughter understood.

"What are you going to do about it?" Ellen asked.

"About this article? Nothing," the king said. When the children expressed their surprise, he explained. "Fortunately, the article has beautiful photographs. The writer is new to the magazine and will get better at descriptive writing with practice. I am going to do something about *your* descriptive writing, however."

"You're giving us a mission," Luke said.

"You already have one, Luke," his father said.

"We do?"

"Yes, you have to write a review of Movie Adventureland after your visit. The marketing department will expect you to write a descriptive review," the king explained.

"That's right!" Kirk agreed. "Is this just a mission for us, or do you want us to send a mission to all the guardians?"

"With or without photographs, descriptive writing is how we experience new places and new things. Every guardian must know how to write descriptively to keep this galaxy strong," the king said.

The three children talked with their father to choose a date to visit Movie Adventureland. They then began working on a mission for the guardians called Descriptive Writing.

What does *protocol* mean?

What are sensory words?

Why didn't the king like the *Best Homes and Gardens* article?

Chapter 29

The king found his children in the media room playing a video game early one afternoon. He stood and watched them for a while before announcing his presence.

"I'm glad you're having fun playing together," he said. "But I just realized that I haven't read your review of Movie Adventureland. You shouldn't **postpone** it. Why don't you show it to me now?"

★ ★ ★ ★ ★ ★ ★ ★ ★ ★
postpone – *delay*
★ ★ ★ ★ ★ ★ ★ ★ ★ ★

Ellen stifled a groan. "We don't have it all done yet. Could we do it later?" she asked in a whiny kind of way.

The king warned her with a glance that it wouldn't be all right to wait.

"I will ask Screen to pull it up for us," Kirk said to be **conciliatory**.

★ ★ ★ ★ ★ ★ ★ ★ ★ ★
conciliatory – *peacemaking*
interminable – *endless*
★ ★ ★ ★ ★ ★ ★ ★ ★ ★

"That's the kind of cooperation I like to see," the king said, smiling.

Kirk asked Screen to end the game and bring up the webpage with the first part of the review in draft. Kirk began reading the beginning of the article aloud.

The new theme park called Movie Adventureland is like being in the movies, only better. The racing, neon lights; the scent of buttery popcorn; and the laughter and screams of thrilled kids meet you at the front entrance and draw you into the park.

The first ride you'll encounter is Jurassic Galaxy. The line for this popular ride snaked around for more than 100 meters during our visit. The ecstatic yet terrified children stood in line impatiently. The parents drew kids' attention to colorful movie posters and rubbery, miniature dinosaurs while they waited. The crowd seemed electrified with excitement about what lay ahead, and we were no different. The sign advertising the **interminable** wait time did not seem to put these families off.

"Stop!" the king said. "The review is all wrong," the king said.

"The review is all wrong?" Ellen said. "The review has the description you asked us for," she said indignantly.

"The review does have appropriate amounts of description," the king said. "The description is well done, in fact."

"The review has description, so what is the problem?" Luke asked.

"The sentences in the review all begin the same way," the king said.

"The sentences all begin with a capital letter, and that is correct, right?" Luke asked.

"The sentences do begin with a capital letter and it is correct to start every sentence with a capital letter," the king agreed.

"The sentences are descriptive and they begin with a capital letter, so I don't understand what the problem is," Ellen said, pouting.

"The sentences all begin with the word *the*," the king said.

"The sentences all beginning with the word *the* is a problem?" Kirk asked. "The number of times *the* is used is the problem?"

"The number of sentences beginning with the word *the* is not the issue. The sentences all start the same way," the king explained.

"The problem is the word *the*?" Ellen asked, frowning.

"The problem is not the word *the*," the king said, frustrated. "The problem is the way the sentences begin."

"The, the, the problem I'm having is I keep beginning everything I say with *the*, even if I don't want to," Ellen said, eyes wide.

"The, the, the problem you describe is my problem too," the king said, clearly alarmed. "The research I want you to do," he said, speaking to Screen, "is to report any unusual happenings on planet Sentence.

Screen began a search and responded, "The Sentence Relays are ongoing at this hour, Your Highness."

"The Sentence Relays?" the king inquired.

"The Sentence Relays are a race to determine the fastest sentences on the planet. The word *the* was chosen to lead the relays as it has the most experience beginning sentences."

"The Sentence Relays are causing the problem, aren't they, Father?" Kirk asked.

"The Sentence Relays are likely to be the cause of our speaking difficulty and the reason your review is written the way it is," the king answered. He attempted to request that *The Guidebook to Grammar Galaxy* be brought to him in the media room. When he stammered, he decided to lead the three children to the castle library instead. There, he withdrew the guidebook and read them the article on sentence starters.

Sentence Starters

There are a number of ways to begin a sentence to keep your readers' interest. Rather than beginning with an article adjective (a, an, the) or the subject of the sentence, try beginning your sentence with:

- **an adverb** *Slowly* the man backed away from the bear.
- **a prepositional phrase** *At the start of the game*, the kids got along well.
- **a participle** *Gasping* for breath, the swimmer emerged from the water.
- **two adjectives** *Cold and hungry*, the skier entered the warm cabin.
- **transition words** *Third*, let the paint dry for eight hours.
- **subordinating conjunctions** *Whether* it rains or not, we are having the picnic.

These sentence starters will keep your writing from sounding repetitive.

"The guidebook makes sense," Kirk said.

"The sentences in our review all begin with *the*," Ellen said. "The article as written will be boring."

"The article will be boring, even though we added a lot of description," Luke agreed.

"The article does need revision, and the sentence order for the relays has to be changed," the king said.

Screen interjected, "The order for the sentences in the competition is pre-determined."

"The order for the sentences is going to have to be changed," the king said firmly. "The plan is to have you three children—"

Ellen completed his thought. "The plan is to get the guardians' help choosing new sentence starters," Ellen said, smiling.

"The conclusion here is that we should send out a mission called Sentence Starters as soon as possible," Kirk added. The three English children got to work and used the space porter to leave for planet Sentence.

What does *postpone* mean?

What is another sentence starter besides *the*?

Why was the word *the* starting the relay for each sentence?

Chapter 30

The royal family was outside playing tennis together. Their problem with reflexive pronouns was behind them. A new player rotated in after every game, so they could all have a turn.

Kirk hit a ball wide into the alley. The king ran for it and was able to just hit it so that it was **lofted** high over the net. The queen hit the ball to the king's part of the court to win the point.

★ ★ ★ ★ ★ ★ ★ ★ ★
lofted – *launched*
★ ★ ★ ★ ★ ★ ★ ★ ★

The king was irritated. "Luke, you have to cover me when I'm pulled off the court."

"She hit it to your side of the court!" Luke said, defending himself.

"I know it's my side of the court, but I had to run out wide to return Kirk's ball. You should have moved over so the court wasn't wide open for them."

Luke nodded but seemed unaffected by the instruction.

The king then served to Kirk, who returned the shot right past Luke at the net. The king tried to return it late and his ball hit the net. "Luke, that was your shot," the king said.

"How was it my shot?" Luke argued.

"You could have put your racket out and hit a winner. Instead, you let it come to me, and we lost the game."

Luke glowered. "I'm going to go take Comet for a walk. Ellen can play for me," Luke said.

The king glanced at the queen to see if she approved. "Let him go," she murmured. "You were a bit hard on him, dear," she added.

The king sighed. She was probably right.

The four of them continued to play. The king tried to be more encouraging of his family's tennis skills.

Later that afternoon when they were having cookies and lemonade, the king apologized to Luke. "I get too upset about tennis," he admitted.

"That's okay, Father," Luke said. "I should listen to you more. You're a great player."

The king beamed and side hugged his son.

The next day Ellen came to the king complaining that Luke's part of their Movie Adventureland review wasn't done. "We decided we would divide up writing the review. We have a deadline, and he keeps making excuses," Ellen said.

"I see," the king said, stroking his beard. He was tempted to tell Luke he would lose a privilege if he didn't get his writing done. But then he thought about his children having to work with others in the future. He wouldn't be able to discipline their coworkers.

"Ellen, I suggest you and Kirk have a meeting with Luke to discuss it," the king said.

Ellen was surprised by her father's response. "Aren't you going to punish him?" she asked.

"You three need to work this out," the king said resolutely.

Ellen left to find Kirk and tell him what their father had said. Kirk agreed they should talk with Luke. They found him in his room reading.

"Luke, we need to talk with you about the resort review," Kirk began.

"Yes, Father is going to punish you if you don't get it done," Ellen warned.

"Did he say that? I thought he just said we had to work it out with him," Kirk said.

Ellen scowled. "Well, he'll probably punish you if you don't cooperate with us," she said.

"I haven't had time to do it," Luke said, defending himself.

"You're reading right now!" Ellen exclaimed. "There's no reason you can't do it today."

Luke's eyes flashed with anger. "You don't know what I'm doing or what I have to do."

Kirk tried to **negotiate** peace. "Luke, do you have time to start on the review today?"

★ ★ ★ ★ ★ ★ ★ ★ ★

negotiate – *discuss*

★ ★ ★ ★ ★ ★ ★ ★ ★

"Maybe," he said **defiantly**.
"Yes," he said after seeing Ellen's reaction. "I'll get it done this afternoon."

defiantly – *rebelliously*

"Wonderful!" Ellen said, leaving his bedchamber in a huff.

"You'd better get it done, Luke. If I were you, I'd be more afraid of her than Father," he joked, gesturing to their sister.

Luke laughed. "Okay. I'll do it."

That evening, Luke sent his finished portion of the review to Kirk. Kirk messaged him via his communicator, "Way to go!" He added Luke's portion of the review to his own and Ellen's.

He looked it over and realized his father would love to see that they'd worked out their problem with Luke. He would probably also want to make sure the review had enough description and used a variety of sentence starters. He sent the review to his father and went to find him to go over it.

"I'm so proud of you three for working together on this, Kirk," the king said when Kirk approached him in his office. "I'm happy to look over your work. But I'm sure you did a fine job!"

He began reading and Kirk noted he was smiling. Then he frowned, smiled, and frowned again. When his father was finished reading, Kirk asked, "What's wrong?"

"Each of you did a good job of writing the review," the king said.

"That's a relief," Kirk said, smiling.

"But," the king said grimly, "it looks like three separate reviews that have been stuck together. I realize now that I haven't taught you how to write with a partner. Call your brother and sister and have them meet us in the library."

When Luke and Ellen joined them, the king began reading the article called "Writing with a Partner" in *The Guide to Grammar Galaxy*.

Writing with a Partner

Writing with a partner can improve your writing and be fun. But writing with a partner can also produce conflict.

To have a good writing partnership:

-Agree on a meeting schedule. Decide on times to meet and what must be accomplished between meetings. If possible, meet in person. Otherwise, decide how you will discuss your writing project.

-Write separately, without concern for what your writing partner will think. Edit your work so it is ready for your partner to review at your next meeting.

-Edit together. Have each writer read his or her own work while the partner actively listens. After listening, the partner should respond with positive comments such as "I noticed," "I felt," or "I pictured."

To help the writer improve, the partner should make statements that begin with "Say more about..." or "Can you explain...?" Make changes together as a result of these discussions.

-Write with one voice. Work written by more than one person may have multiple styles or voices. To give your work a unified style, have one partner go through the piece and add personal touches.

-Do a final edit. Read through the work together after one partner has written the piece in one voice. Make any spelling, punctuation, or grammar changes needed.

"It's kind of like doubles in tennis, isn't it, Father?" Luke asked. "You can't just play your own game. You have to help your partner."

"You've got it exactly, Luke!" the king said proudly.

"We didn't use one voice in writing our review. It sounds like three voices!" Kirk said.

"Would you two be willing to let me use my voice in writing the review?" Ellen asked.

"Is that less work for me? If so, sure!" Luke joked. The rest of the family laughed.

"Ellen, we need to meet to edit the review together first," Kirk said.

Ellen nodded. "If we didn't know how to write a paper with other people, I bet the guardians don't know either. Let's write a mission called Writing with a Partner."

"That's my girl!" the king said.

What does *negotiate* mean?

What is one of the steps in writing with a partner?

Why didn't the king like his children's review?

Chapter 31

The king noticed that Ellen seemed down at the dinner table. "What is wrong, young lady?" he asked.

"Nothing," Ellen answered glumly.

The king caught the queen's eye. The queen indicated that she would take over. "Ellen, you've hardly touched your dessert and it's one of your favorites," she said gently.

"I'm just not hungry I guess."

"She is upset about our resort review," Luke said.

Ellen shot a warning glance at Luke. "I am not!" she declared a little too loudly.

"I explained to her that it will take time for the search engine to show our review to more people," Kirk said.

"So you haven't had many people read your review yet?" the queen asked.

Ellen shook her head. "All that work for nothing," she said ruefully.

"Ellen, you three learned to write descriptively, vary your sentence starters, and write as a team. I wouldn't call that nothing," the king said as gently as he could.

"It's just disappointing. That's all," Ellen said, sighing.

174

"Give it time, Ellen. You will get more people reading your review soon. I'm sure of it," the queen said, smiling confidently.

Ellen's face brightened a little.

"I told you so!" Luke said. "We'll be famous reviewers before you know it." Ellen laughed despite trying to maintain a pout. "If you're not going to finish that dessert, may I have it?" Luke asked innocently.

"Forget it, Luke. It's mine," Ellen said, plunging her fork into the dessert.

Several days later the king walked past Ellen's bedchamber door. and saw her in her room styling her hair.

"Any progress on the number of readers for your resort review?" the king asked her hopefully.

"No, and we wanted to talk to you about it," Ellen said **earnestly**.

★ ★ ★ ★ ★ ★ ★ ★ ★ ★

earnestly – *seriously*

★ ★ ★ ★ ★ ★ ★ ★ ★ ★

"Okay, what is it?"

"I know Grammar Galaxy Kids is a new website and it takes time to get people to visit the site. But it's like no one is seeing it. We suspect that the Gremlin is blocking access to the site."

The king's face registered alarm. "Oh, no! I didn't think of that. Search engines can exercise a lot of control over what people see. It would be the perfect way for the Gremlin to interfere. Don't worry, Ellen. I'll check into it."

Ellen nodded gratefully. The king left her bedchamber determined to find out why his children's website was not being viewed.

His first step was to ask Screen to connect him with the CEO of Groogle. The CEO was friendly and seemed happy to hear from the king.

"How may I be of service?" he asked.

The king explained that his children had begun a new website. He noted that their first post, a review of the new Movie Adventureland resort, had gotten no views whatsoever.

"How long has the site been live?" the CEO asked.

"I believe Kirk made the site live three weeks ago, and the post was published a week after that."

"Your Highness, it takes time for our search engine to track new content."

"I understand that. That's what I told my children. But it seems odd that there have been no visits to the site."

"I will take a look at their site right now," the CEO said. He shared his screen with the king and momentarily the Grammar Galaxy Kids webpage appeared. The first and only article they had published appeared on the screen as well. "I think I see the problem," the CEO said.

"You do?" the king said. "Has the Gremlin somehow blocked access to the site?" he asked, beginning to get angry.

"I don't think that's the issue, your Majesty. Rather, I think this title is the problem."

"The title? What's wrong with it? It's capitalized and spelled appropriately," he noted.

"Yes, it is. But it's not very **compelling**. New Resort Review doesn't tell people that it is about Movie Adventureland. And it doesn't

★ ★ ★ ★ ★ ★ ★ ★ ★ ★
compelling – *irresistible*
★ ★ ★ ★ ★ ★ ★ ★ ★ ★

make the resort sound intriguing at all." The CEO stopped talking and appeared to be reading the review. "That's too bad because this is an excellent review. I know kids in the galaxy will want to visit the resort after reading this. One thing we can do is increase your ranking in the search engine with a paid advertisement."

"Paid? I know the kids don't have an advertising budget for their site," the king responded. "But I do appreciate the offer. I would like to have the kids write a new title for the article and see if that makes a difference."

"Very wise. Let's search and see what has been published about the resort already." The CEO did a quick search and a number of results appeared on the screen. "Their review could benefit from the inclusion of some words like *thrill*, *exciting*, or *action-packed*. You'll want to make sure that their website and review are using good SEO."

SEO. The king reddened a bit as he realized he had no idea what SEO was. He didn't want to appear the fool, so he simply nodded and thanked the CEO for his time.

"Any time, Your Majesty," the CEO said, ending the call.

The king used his communicator to ask his three children to come to his office. He asked them to pick up *The Guidebook to Grammar Galaxy* in the castle library first.

When the three arrived, Luke asked, "What's wrong now? What has the Gremlin done this time?"

The king raised his eyebrow and said, "As a matter of fact, nothing. This latest problem is a result of your **negligence**."

★ ★ ★ ★ ★ ★ ★ ★ ★ ★
negligence – *failure*
★ ★ ★ ★ ★ ★ ★ ★ ★ ★

"Okay. What did Kirk and Ellen do now?" Luke joked.

Kirk and Ellen looked annoyed but were more interested in what their father had to say.

"I just spoke with the CEO of Groogle. He looked up your website to see if the Gremlin was blocking access. He found something very interesting."

"A hacker?" Kirk asked.

"No. In fact, let's look at your website right now." Screen pulled up the website and Kirk commented that it looked fine.

"Groogle's CEO showed me your title in comparison to other articles about Movie Adventureland. If you were a kid, would your title 'New Resort Review' make you want to read it?" the king asked.

"Well, I do like resorts. And new resorts are always cool," Luke said defensively.

The king asked Screen to search for Movie Adventureland. Screen immediately produced a list of results.

"Read some of these titles for me, will you?" the king said.

Ellen began reading them aloud.

"I'd much rather go to these resorts then the one we visited," Luke admitted.

"Luke, all of these articles are about the same place we visited," Kirk said.

"That is correct, Kirk. It's just that these titles are much more enticing," the king said.

The three English children nodded. "I want to make sure the three of you know how to write good titles. Luke, will you read the entry on creating titles from the guidebook?" the king asked.

Luke used the table of contents to find the entry and began reading it aloud.

Creating Titles
A good title has three characteristics: 1) interests readers, 2) communicates content, and 3) shares the author's attitude toward the subject. **Creating the best title requires brainstorming.** Respond to these 10 title prompts. Narrow your choice to your top three. Then ask others for their favorite. 　1. Write a title that's a question. 　2. Use a sensory image from your writing as a title. 　3. Write a title beginning with an -ing verb. 　4. Write a one- or two-word title. 　5. Write a three-word title. 　6. Write a four-word title. 　7. Write a five-word title. 　8. Use a common saying or quote as a title. 　9. Change one word in the title from #8. 　10. Put two of these titles together with a colon [:].* 　*Inspired by the University of Minnesota's Writing Center's adaptation of Richard Leahy's "Twenty Titles for the Writer." http://writing.umn.edu/sws/assets/pdf/quicktips/titles.pdf*

"There is one more thing," the king said. "Groogle's CEO said you would want to make sure you are using good SEO for your title. Do you know what that means?"

"Yes!" Kirk said. "It stands for search engine optimization. You have to make sure that your title uses the same words that people are searching for online. Those words are called keywords. Keywords are what we learned to use in the writing and speaking process, remember?"

"Honestly, no," Luke admitted.

"The main words in sentences are called keywords. We wrote the keywords down from a story or article. Then we rewrote it with new vocabulary words," Kirk said.

"And we learned that choosing keywords from a speech can allow us to give a speech without reading it," Ellen added.

"We could have searched for the keywords people are searching for Movie Adventureland. I should have thought of that. I'm sorry, Father," Kirk said.

"Can we do a search for keywords and then write a new title for our review right away?" Ellen asked.

"I don't see why not," Kirk said.

"Does everyone need to know how to write a good title?" Luke asked. "Or is it just famous resort reviewers like us?" he smirked.

"I know just what you're getting at, Luke. Get to work on writing a mission called Creating Titles. Perhaps the guardians could help you choose the best title for your review?" the king said. The three English children loved the idea.

What does *negligence* mean?

What is one idea for writing a good title?

What did the kids think was causing their lack of readers?

Chapter 32

"Hey, El," Kirk said at the open door to his sister's bedchamber.

"Hey," she answered, adjusting a pink bow on Comet's neck. "What's up?"

Kirk frowned at the bow but thought better of bringing it up. He had more important matters to discuss. "We were contacted via the Grammar Galaxy Kids website and I wondered how to respond."

"What did the person say?" Ellen asked, allowing Comet to escape her lap.

"Let me read it to you," Kirk said, looking at his communicator. "Here it is."

Dear Guardians,

I know this isn't English related, but I thought you might be able to help me. I have a younger brother who annoys me all the time. When I start to play a video game, he wants a turn right then. He won't leave me alone when I have a friend over. And he is always making fun of me. What can I do?

Signed,
Frustrated Sister

"Hm. I see why she's frustrated," Ellen said. "Are you thinking we should write her back?"

"I was thinking *you* should write her back. We know how to write together, but it's more work than just one person writing."

"That's true. Okay, I'll write her back."

"Great, El. You can respond from the website."

Ellen got right to work in the castle's computer lab. She loved giving advice. And she certainly knew what it was like to have an annoying younger brother. She thought and wrote, thought and wrote, and was ready to click send on her response. But something stopped her.

What if I made a grammar or spelling mistake? Ellen worried. *I better ask Mother to review it first*, she thought.

She found the queen in her study. "Come in," the queen said. "Oh, Ellen, I'm glad you're here. I just had an amazing idea for a new mystery novel for kids. Twelve kids are invited to spend the night in a new library by a game maker. The kids have to use the clues they're given to escape from the library. Isn't that fantastic?" the queen gushed.

"Yes! I love it! There's just one problem," Ellen said **solemnly**.

"What?"

★ ★ ★ ★ ★ ★ ★ ★ ★ ★
solemnly – *seriously*
★ ★ ★ ★ ★ ★ ★ ★ ★ ★

"That's the plot of the book *Mr. Lemoncello's Library*."

"It is? Oh, dear. I must have heard the plot and thought it was my own idea. Oh, well," the queen said, laughing. "I'll come up with another idea. Now, why are you here? Are you needing something?"

"Yes," Ellen said. She explained about the message they'd received and read it to her mother. "Kirk thought it would be best if I answered her and I did. I was ready to send my answer when I thought I should have you check it first."

"Very wise, Ellen. Would you send what you've written to my computer so I can check it carefully?" Ellen agreed and was able to send her what she'd written via her communicator. Soon the queen was reading Ellen's response via her laptop.

Ellen was encouraged that her mother wasn't making corrections. But when she saw her mother's face, she knew something was wrong.

"What did I do wrong? I did check my spelling and grammar," Ellen said, defending herself.

"The spelling and grammar are fine. But the advice? You told her to put a sign on her door that reads 'No Boys Allowed.'"

Ellen nodded. "Yes, he should remember to stay out."

"You told her to hide the game remotes from him so he can't play unless she wants him to. And worst of all, you advised her to make fun of her brother when her friends are over so he will be sure to leave her alone."

181

"He makes fun of her, so it's only fair," Ellen **retorted**.

retorted – *answered*
scoffed – *made fun of*

"You know this isn't the way to settle conflict. The advice you've given her will make matters worse."

"So, you don't think I should write her?" Ellen asked.

"I'm not saying that. In fact, I think writing her is a splendid idea. But I want your brothers to be a part of it." The queen messaged the two boys to her office and asked the butler to bring her *The Guidebook to Grammar Galaxy*. When the boys arrived, she explained what she and Ellen had discussed.

"You thought putting a 'No Boys Allowed' sign up would work?" Luke **scoffed**. "Wouldn't stop me."

"Luke, we'll return to discussing this particular letter in a moment. But for now, I want to encourage you three to start an advice column."

"What's that?" Luke asked.

"That's why I have the guidebook here. Here's what it says about advice columns."

Advice Column
Advice columns were traditionally published in newspapers and magazines. But they are now a part of a variety of digital media. A usually anonymous reader submits a question about a problem, hoping for advice from the columnist. Advice columnists are referred to as agony aunts and uncles in British English.
Columnists may have an area of expertise, such as medicine or psychology. They may write under a pseudonym or fictitious name. The columnist may actually be a group of writers writing under the same name.

Advice columnists follow these steps to write an effective column:

- **Decide who your audience is.** Consider age, gender, and specific life circumstances. You should have experience or education in answering your audience's questions.

- **Review other advice columns for your audience**. Determine how long and detailed your answers should be.

- **Restate the question.** After beginning with your reader's question, summarize the issue in a sentence. Make sure you also communicate empathy with your reader. For example, "Dealing with a bully can be really hard."

- **Don't lecture.** Your reader may have already made mistakes in trying to solve the problem. Focus on what is to be done going forward.

- **Focus on solving one problem.** Your reader may have numerous questions. Focus on the biggest issue that you can help with.

- **Provide multiple perspectives on the issue.** Consider the needs and feelings of each of the people involved in your reader's problem. To do that, you may need to ask other people for their advice. You may also need to research the best advice for this particular problem. Read your advice to friends and family before publishing it. Even if you are an expert, advise your reader to seek professional help when that's wise. You can't give the best advice when you don't know much about your reader.

- **Write casually.** Read your writing out loud to make sure it sounds natural. You want your reader to easily understand your advice, so avoid jargon.

- **Choose a title that grabs attention.** You want others with the same problem to want to read your article. "Boy Needs Help Convincing Parents to Get Dog" is more engaging than "Parents and Pet Ownership."

- **Proofread your response.** If your answer has grammar and spelling errors, your reader may not respect your advice.

- **Encourage readers to ask questions.** Give your readers a way to contact you to ask questions. If you receive questions apart from your advice column, make sure you get permission to publish the question. Keep the identity of your readers private.

"That sounds like a lot of work!" Luke said.

The queen laughed. "Yes, but it can also be a lot of fun to write an advice column. I used to write one."

"You did?" the kids responded in surprise.

"Yes. I wrote one for single women before I married your father," the queen said. "I got a lot of questions about men. I still haven't figured them out," she said chuckling.

"Can't we just write this girl back without writing a column?" Luke whined.

"You could. But I'm sure many kids in the galaxy want to know how to get along better with brothers and sisters. This way, many people can read your advice. And you'll get excellent writing experience."

"What is our advice for this girl?" Kirk asked. "And couldn't we get too many questions to answer?" Kirk asked.

"Yes, that could happen," the queen answered. "I would like the three of you to help Ellen with advice for Frustrated Sister."

"We could ask the guardians to help, right, Mother?" Ellen suggested.

"I love that idea!" the queen exclaimed. "An advice column written for and by guardians."

The three English children began working on a mission called Advice Column. And the queen tried to come up with a new mystery novel idea.

What does *solemnly* mean?

What's one step in writing a good advice column?

What was wrong with Ellen's advice?

Galactic Robotics Conference

Chapter 33

Kirk read the letter the butler had given him and smiled. He hadn't been this excited since his team had taken first place in the robotics competition. He had to tell his father.

"Guess what?" he said, finding his father in his study.

The king hesitated for a moment before determining that Kirk was in a good mood. "What?"

"I've been invited to submit a research paper to the *Galactic Robotics Journal*," he said proudly.

"That's fantastic!" the king said, standing and hugging his son.

"And there's more. They want me to present at the Galactic Robotics Conference." Kirk grinned at his father's enthusiastic response to this news.

"Kirk, I'm so proud of you! I just hope you don't expect me to help you. I'm not much of an expert on robotics," the king said.

Kirk laughed. "No, I know. I'm on my own."

"You'll do a great job. We need to celebrate. I'll tell Cook to prepare your favorites."

That evening at dinner, the conversation was all about the honor **bestowed** upon Kirk. The family discussed the interesting people he would meet and how much he would learn at the conference.

★ ★ ★ ★ ★ ★ ★ ★ ★ ★
bestowed – *given*
★ ★ ★ ★ ★ ★ ★ ★ ★ ★

"When will you start writing?" the queen asked.

185

"Right away. I'm excited about it, and it's best to get an early start, I think."

The queen smiled, proud of her **diligent** son.

After a delicious meal, Kirk asked to be excused. He couldn't wait to begin. He went to the

★ ★ ★ ★ ★ ★ ★ ★ ★ ★

diligent – *hardworking*
potential – *possible*

★ ★ ★ ★ ★ ★ ★ ★ ★ ★

computer lab and put his fingers on the keyboard. *What should I write about?* he wondered. Many ideas came to him. Robotics was a broad field with numerous areas of research.

As he considered each topic that came to mind, he shook his head. His paper had to be perfect. This paper would be published in a prestigious journal. He couldn't afford to write anything that wasn't accurate. He couldn't write about anything that was obvious to the journal's audience either. He wasn't writing for kids but adults. On the other hand, he *was* a kid. And though he knew a lot about robotics, there was so much technical information he didn't know.

He thought and he thought about **potential** topics, but nothing seemed like the perfect one for him. He finally decided to go to bed. He hoped some sleep would help him come up with the right idea.

The next day he returned to the computer lab. The computer screen seemed to taunt him. *Don't you have an idea yet?* He reviewed ideas he'd had the day before. But they still seemed either too basic, too boring, or too technical for him to write about. He realized he had plenty of time and was probably putting too much pressure on himself to come up with a topic. He decided to wait until something came to him.

A couple of weeks went by and Kirk still hadn't chosen a topic. He started to feel anxious about it. When the king asked him how the writing was going, he responded angrily that he had plenty of time. The king was taken aback.

"Yes, you have time, but I thought you wanted to get a good start on your paper. I wasn't trying to upset you," the king explained.

Kirk sighed. It was so embarrassing, but he decided to admit the truth. "I don't know how to choose a topic for my paper. I've tried and nothing seems right. It has to be the perfect topic, or I'll make a fool of myself."

"Hold on there, Kirk. No wonder you've been having trouble. It does not have to be the perfect topic. There is no such thing. You just need a good topic to write about," the king said empathetically.

"I just don't want to look stupid. These are smart people I look up to. I don't even know how to choose a good topic. I'm doomed," Kirk moaned.

The king smiled. "You're not doomed. Remember when I said I couldn't help you with your paper?" Kirk nodded. "I was wrong. I can help you choose a good topic."

"You can?" Kirk responded with excitement.

"Yes."

Then Kirk became skeptical. "How can you help me choose a good topic when you don't know much about robotics?"

"Because there are principles for choosing a good research paper topic, regardless of what you're writing about. In fact, your brother and sister need to hear this too. Have them meet us in the library in a few."

Kirk obeyed his father and Luke and Ellen arrived, ready to hear why their father had called them.

"What's the crisis now?" Luke asked.

"Nothing," Kirk said with a guilty expression.

"Ooh, what did Kirk do wrong?" Luke asked, happy that he wasn't in trouble.

"Kirk hasn't done anything wrong," the king said sternly. "I called you here to teach you how to choose a topic for a research paper."

"You don't have a topic yet?" Luke gasped. Kirk glared at him.

"Luke, you seem to be enjoying Kirk's difficulty in choosing a topic. So you can join him. You'll be writing a research paper too. And, Ellen, although you haven't been teasing Kirk, I want you to have the experience as well. I'm going to read about how to choose a topic from *The Guidebook to Grammar Galaxy*."

How to Choose a Research Paper Topic

To find the right research paper topic, do some library research. An encyclopedia or reference book can give you some ideas. When you find one, ask yourself if the topic:

- **interests you.** If it bores you, you won't write a good paper. It's also likely that your audience will be bored too.

- **is somewhat familiar.** You can write about a completely new topic. But you'll have less work if you already know something about the subject.

- **is appropriate for the audience.** Does it match the guidelines your teacher or publication has given you? Will your reader be able to understand it?

- **has enough written about it and not too much.** Search the library's catalog for books on the subject. Ask your teacher's or librarian's help in finding more resources in the library and online.

A topic like space with too much written about it is too broad. Choose a specific part of the topic like the planet Saturn to write about. A topic with few references is too narrow. You will have difficulty writing a paper of 3-5 pages. Expand the topic or choose another.

- **is better than another topic you find.** Be willing to change topics if you find one more interesting, familiar, appropriate, or with more sources.

After considering potential topics, be willing to choose a good topic rather than a perfect one. Perfectionism can keep you from getting started on your research paper.

"Hm. I don't know what my topic is, but I'm excited to start looking for one!" Kirk said after the king finished reading.

"Me too! I'd like to look for a topic right now," Ellen added.

"Now?" Luke groaned.

"There's no time like the present," the king said cheerfully. "Why don't you three head to the main library branch and start researching?"

"It will be fun, Luke. You'll be reading about what interests you," Ellen said.

"As hungry as I am, I'm only interested in reading cookbooks," Luke joked. The rest of the family laughed.

"I could do with some lunch myself," the king said. "But I think we should send the guardians a mission called Choosing a Research Paper Topic first. Everyone has to write research papers, and choosing a topic can be tough without help."

The children agreed and worked together to create the mission.

What does *bestowed* mean?

What's one characteristic of a good research paper topic?

Why was Kirk putting off choosing a topic for his paper?

Chapter 34

The king found Kirk in the computer lab, surrounded by printed sheets of paper. "What's all this?" he asked.

"Oh, this is for my research paper," Kirk said proudly.

The king picked up some of the papers and skimmed them. "Pretty interesting stuff!"

"I know! The head librarian helped me find enough material on robot pets."

"That's wonderful! I'm so pleased that you're making progress." Kirk beamed, happy that his father was proud of him. The king patted Kirk on the shoulder. "I'm going to see how your brother and sister are coming along," he said, leaving the computer lab.

The king found Ellen in her bedchamber, surrounded by books. When her father asked about them, she explained, "They're for my research paper on the Lipizzan horse. Did you know it's the horse of royalty?"

"I *did* know that."

"Why don't we own any? We only have Quarter horses. Could we buy some? They're so beautiful! Please!" she pleaded.

"I don't know about that," the king said haltingly.

"You'll read my report and you'll know we have to have Lipizzans!" Ellen exclaimed.

"Hold your horses there, young lady!" the king chuckled at his pun. "I know you're excited, but Lipizzans are expensive."

"The price depends on their health, training, and show experience."

"I'm impressed you know that," the king said.

"You'll really be impressed when you read my report. Then you'll want to buy these beautiful horses for sure."

The king couldn't help but smile at his daughter's enthusiasm. "We'll see," he said. "For now, it looks like you have work to do."

The king left Ellen and went to find Luke. He found him in the game room, playing a virtual reality game. "What are you doing?" he asked, startling Luke.

"Oh, hi, Father. I'm working on my research paper," he said **unmoved**. He removed the headset he was wearing.

"You are," the king said in a **sardonic** tone.

★ ★ ★ ★ ★ ★ ★ ★ ★ ★
unmoved – *unaffected*
sardonic – *mocking*
justifying – *defending*
★ ★ ★ ★ ★ ★ ★ ★ ★ ★

"Yes! For real!" Luke said, **justifying** himself. "My paper is on the history of virtual reality gaming. I wanted to play this old game to compare the quality to what we have today."

"Where did you get this game?"

"The library. I found it by doing a search for virtual reality. Do you want to play?" Luke offered.

"Uh, not right now. Are you making progress on your paper then?" the king asked, eyebrows raised.

"Yes! I just have a few more old VR games to play."

"More games?" the king asked disapprovingly.

"Yes. I have to know what the first games were like, don't I?"

The king was surprised to find himself agreeing. "But you do have to write a paper too," he said.

"I know and I will," Luke promised cheerfully. He put his headset back on.

The king shook his head and smiled, thinking that Luke reminded him of himself at that age.

A week later the king asked for a status report on the papers at dinner. He didn't miss their discomfort at answering the question.

"I have all the information…" Kirk said.

"I do too!" Ellen agreed.

"I've played all the games," Luke added.

"But what?" the king asked.

"I've tried to write the paper and it's just…" Kirk began.

"Overwhelming," Ellen finished for him. "There's so much to say."

"Okay, I haven't tried to write the paper, but I'm overwhelmed too. Where do you start?" Luke said.

"You have taught them how to take notes, haven't you, dear? And you explained outlines?" the queen asked her husband.

"Uh, I think I have…" he stuttered.

"You haven't," Ellen said. The king glared at her playfully for tattling on him.

"Dear, I'm surprised at you. These poor children must have been so stressed and confused," she said, looking at them sympathetically. "Straight away after dinner, I'll teach you children everything you need to know." The kids nodded appreciatively. "Come to think of it, I'm *not* surprised at you," she told her husband. "You have always tried to write without proper note-taking and outlining." She gave him a tsk-tsk and the king looked a little ashamed.

After dinner, the queen led her children to the castle library. She read them the articles in *The Guidebook to Grammar Galaxy* on taking notes and outlining.

Taking Notes for a Research Paper

Before taking notes for a research paper, decide the three to five main points your paper will make.

To make this decision, skim the reference material you've collected. Write down the main topics covered in each, which are typically in bold or subheadings. Choose the most important and interesting topics. You may need to combine topics.

For example, in researching the giant panda, you may find information about:
– habitat
– diet
– teeth
– weight/size
– speed
– population
– how pandas are being protected
– relatives
– species
– behavior
– babies' growth

To limit your paper to three to five topics with enough material, you may create a main point called General Information. Under General Information, you may include information about the size, species, and habitat of pandas.

Your second point might be called Life of Pandas. You can include information about growth of baby pandas, diet, as well as behavior of adults.

Your third point could be Protecting Pandas. Here you can discuss population, threats, and how the Giant Panda is being protected.

When taking notes, you'll ignore information that doesn't add to the main points you'll be writing about. With your Giant Panda paper, you won't take notes on their teeth, speed, or relatives.

The two most common ways of taking notes are using note cards or a digital note-taking program. Both methods require you to use the following steps to take good notes.

1) Write down detailed information about the sources you are using. Include author name, book/article title, the name of the magazine or newspaper, or website URL. Include the publisher and place and date of publication if known. In the case of printed works, also write the location of the source (e.g., library). This will be helpful if you need to return to it. Number each source card so you can save time writing the number with your notes, rather than the source title.

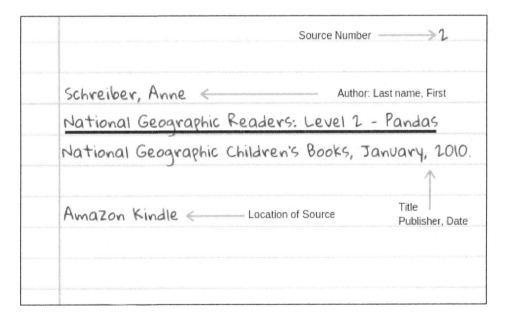

2) Add ONE fact or idea to each note, using abbreviations, keywords, or drawings. Your note should include:
  – the source card number
  – the order of the note, using letters (the second card from source 1 would be labeled 1B)
  – the subject of the note, including the main point it will support
  – the fact or information (being careful to include quotation marks if taken word for word from the source)
  – the page number on which the information was found if any.

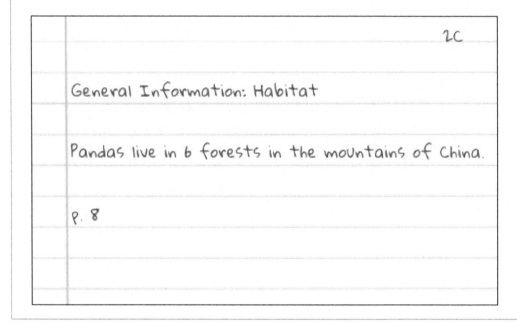

"We'll have tons of cards if we write just one fact on a card, won't we?" Luke asked.

"You will have quite a few cards, yes," the queen agreed.

"But won't all the notes be just as overwhelming as the books and articles we have?" Ellen asked.

"They could be without an outline," the queen said. She turned to the article on outlining in the guidebook and read it aloud.

Outlining a Research Paper

A research paper has three main parts: an introduction, body, and a conclusion. **The introduction includes an interesting fact, quote, or story that grabs the reader's attention.** The introduction also includes the thesis statement, which is like a paragraph's topic sentence. It tells the reader what the research paper is about. It also communicates the main points of the paper.

The body of the research paper gives information on three to five main points. The conclusion of the paper summarizes the information in the body, restates the thesis in a new way, and may refer back to the introduction to bring the paper to a close.

An outline helps you to organize your research paper notes into this structure. Nearly any research paper can be outlined using the format below. Note that the structure of the outline moves from Roman numerals to capital letters to numbers. Further details can be added using lowercase letters and then lowercase Roman numerals.

I. Introduction
  A. Interesting fact, quote, story
  B. Thesis statement
  C. Main points of paper

II. Body
  A. Main point #1
    1. Fact or detail #1
    2. Fact or detail #2
    3. Fact or detail #3
  B. Main point #2
    1. Fact or detail #1
    2. Fact or detail #2
    3. Fact or detail #3
  C. Main point #3
    1. Fact or detail #1
    2. Fact or detail #2
    3. Fact or detail #3

III. Conclusion
  A. Summary of Body
  B. Restatement of thesis
  C. Refer back to introduction

"Using the Giant Panda paper example, you would decide the order of facts you want to write about under General Information," the queen said.

"Are we only writing three facts for each main point?" Kirk asked.

"Not necessarily," the queen said. "This outline is just an example. You may have ten things you want to write about under General Information and five under Life of Pandas."

"This seems like a lot of extra work. Can't I just start writing my paper?" Luke asked.

The queen sighed. "Many people think that way, Luke. But you will do the work ahead of time or you will do the work while writing your paper. Without an outline, you will spend a lot of time trying to remember the most important information and where it came from. Believe it or not, a good outline will save you time."

Luke appeared unconvinced, but Ellen was enthusiastic. "I love organizing. Thanks for sharing this with us, Mother," she said, hugging her.

Luke groaned that her sister was saying what their mother wanted to hear, and the queen noticed. "Luke, I encourage you to try note-taking and outlining before you decide it's not worth it. As you continue in your studies, your research papers will be longer. You'll find it hard to share a lot of information without an outline," she said.

Luke agreed that he would give it a try and then thought of something. "Hey! The guardians are writing research papers too, right? They should know about taking notes and outlining."

"Absolutely!" the queen said, smiling at her youngest. "While it's fresh in your minds, why don't you three send out a mission on the topic?"

The English children got to work on the mission before beginning their own note-taking and outlining.

What does *sardonic* mean?

How many facts should be on each note card?

Why did the queen say Luke should try creating an outline?

Chapter 35

"Your research paper on robotic pets is **enthralling**!" the king told Kirk as he finished reviewing it on his computer.

★ ★ ★ ★ ★ ★ ★ ★ ★
enthralling – *fascinating*
★ ★ ★ ★ ★ ★ ★ ★ ★

"You really think so?" Kirk asked, beaming.

"I do indeed. And your grammar, spelling, vocabulary, and composition look good too. You started every sentence with a capital letter. There are end marks and no run-on sentences. I even noticed a few correctly used semicolons! You used strong vocabulary words with the right shades of meaning. You didn't use the wrong homonym. You used a variety of sentence starters. And you chose a fantastic title! There's just one more thing you'll have to add," the king said.

"What is that?" Kirk asked.

"Source citations."

"What are source citations?"

"You know the information your mother had you note for each reference you used? You'll share that within the paper. You'll also list your references at the end of the paper," the king explained.

"Oh, okay. That shouldn't be too hard."

"No, not with the good notes you took," the king agreed. "Let me see your paper again when you've added the references. Then you should be ready to submit it to the *Galactic Robotics Journal*," he said, smiling.

Kirk thanked his father for his help with the paper. As soon as the king left the computer lab, Kirk got to work adding the citations. He referred to his note cards and added the information about his sources. By dinner time, he was finished and happy he had the work done.

When the family was about to leave the dining room for read-aloud time, Kirk asked if his father could check his citations first. The king happily agreed. He asked the rest of the family to wait at the table for him until he was finished looking the paper over.

The king began reading aloud what Kirk had written. "Robotic seals are being used as pets in hospitals and nursing facilities across the galaxy. I found this information on the *Galactic News* website." The king's eye's widened; he was **stunned** by what he'd read.

Kirk reacted to the king's surprise. "That's my source for what I wrote about **therapeutic** pets. Is that a problem?"

★ ★ ★ ★ ★ ★ ★ ★ ★ ★
stunned – *shocked*
therapeutic – *healing*
★ ★ ★ ★ ★ ★ ★ ★ ★ ★

"No, your source is fine, but that isn't how you cite a source in your paper," the king explained sternly.

Kirk's face reddened with embarrassment. The queen noticed immediately and asked her husband if he had told Kirk how to cite references.

"Well, I—, I said he had to cite them!" the king said, defending himself.

"That means no, he didn't tell him how," Ellen interjected. She and Luke chuckled.

"How on English can you expect this boy to know how to properly cite a reference if you don't tell him?" the queen asked indignantly.

"I just thought he would know!" the king said.

"Were you born knowing how to cite a reference?" the queen asked, her eyes narrowed. The king hung his head in shame. "I'm going to teach these children right now," she said. She had Kirk, Luke, and Ellen follow her to the castle library.

When they arrived, she had Kirk read the entry on citing references in *The Guidebook to Grammar Galaxy*.

Citing References

Information in a paper that comes from a reference such as a book, magazine, newspaper, website, or another source must be cited or credited. An exception to citations is when information is common knowledge that is presented in numerous sources. A second exception is when you are summarizing previously cited information. When in doubt, cite the reference.

There are two places references are listed in a paper: 1) in the text with the information from that source; and 2) in a list at the end of a paper. References listed in the text must appear in the final list, and references at the end of the paper should appear in the text.

The way references are cited is determined by the style guide used. Your teacher or publication may give you the style to use. MLA (Modern Language Association) is most commonly used for language arts and cultural studies. APA (American Psychological Association) is most commonly used for psychology, education, and the sciences. Chicago (Chicago Manual of Style) is used most often for business, history, and fine arts. See the following chart for the main differences in style. However, note that style guides are always being updated. Check a recent style guide or use a digital tool to correctly format sources in your list.

	MLA	APA	Chicago
Publications using	Language arts Cultural studies	Psychology/Science Education	Business History/Fine Arts
In-text reference	(Wilson, 188-189) Wilson argued (188-189).	(Wilson, 2019) (Wilson, 2019, p. 188) – *direct quotes only*	(Wilson 2019, 188) or Wilson argued.[2] – *source cited on page*
Source list page name	Works Cited	References	Bibliography, Works Cited, Literature Cited – *optional*
Title page	On page 1, top left: Your Name Instructor Name Course Date Center title	Separate title page, upper half: Title Author Name Institution/School Top left: Running Head: SHORT VERSION OF TITLE	Separate title page Title Author Publisher & Location
Page numbers	Upper right corner: Your Last Name, 1	Upper left corner: Short version of title Upper right corner: 1	Include page numbers: 1

Luke looked at the information in the table and was worried. "That makes no sense to me!" he declared.

"It won't make sense now," his mother said reassuringly. "It will make sense when we start formatting your paper."

"Will I be using APA style because my paper is in the sciences?" Kirk asked.

"You will need to check with the editor of the *Galactic Robotics Journal*, but I think so," the queen answered.

"It says we have to check the style guide. What does that mean?" Ellen asked.

"Every year on planet Composition, there is a style guide show. It has the latest fashion in citation and formatting. Screen, show us the most recent Style Guide show," the queen requested.

Screen started a video with models showing off the new guidelines for MLA, APA, and Chicago style. Ellen was fascinated but Luke groaned. "I can't believe they film this stuff!" he said.

Ellen rolled her eyes and asked her mother what style guide she should use for her paper on horses. "Normally I would say APA, but why don't you use MLA? Luke, you can use Chicago style." When Luke started to complain again, the queen cut him off. "Luke, when I was your age, I had to type my citations myself. You have it much easier with digital tools that will format your paper for you. So no more complaining," she warned.

Luke apologized and the queen thanked him with a hug.

"I want to get to work adding correctly formatted citations to my paper. But first I think we have to explain this to the guardians," Kirk said.

The queen thought that was a wonderful idea. She worked with the three English children to create a mission called Citing References.

What does *enthralling* mean?

What are the three citation styles the kids learned about?

What did Kirk do wrong in citing his source?

Chapter 36

"I'm going to redo a whole section of the garden," the king announced to the queen one morning.

"Oh?" the queen said in surprise. "I think it looks beautiful as is."

"Yes, yes, but I saw some garden photos online that I love. I know our garden can be even more spectacular."

"You've been looking at garden photos online?" the queen asked in disbelief.

"Yes! You're not the only one in this family who looks for inspiration online," the king said, defending himself.

"Okay, well, that's wonderful. Do you have pictures to show me?"

The king responded by having Screen produce the photos he'd saved.

"That garden is magnificent!" the queen exclaimed. "But it looks like a huge project to me."

"Oh, it is," the king said. "But it will be well worth it."

The queen shook her head and smiled. She suspected that he would regret taking on the project once the hard work started. But she didn't say anything to **dampen** his enthusiasm.

★ ★ ★ ★ ★ ★ ★ ★ ★ ★

dampen – *reduce*

★ ★ ★ ★ ★ ★ ★ ★ ★ ★

A few days later, Kirk was looking for his father. He hoped to talk with him about his upcoming talk at the Galactic Robotics Conference. He learned that the king was outside, hard at work on his garden project.

When Kirk joined him in a flower bed, the king was happy to see him. He stood up to take a break and have a drink of water. "It's coming along, Kirk!" he said. "I don't think I've shown you the plan. This is a picture of what I'm trying to achieve," the king said, showing Kirk the image on his communicator.

"Wow! That's an amazing garden!" Kirk exclaimed about the photo. "You have a lot of work left to do though," he said, looking around him.

The king sighed, realizing his son was right, and then had a thought. "Kirk, why don't you help me? You'll be king one day and you'll want to add something special to the gardens. You need to know how to do **landscaping**. It's good to get your hands dirty," the king said, showing off hands covered in soil.

★ ★ ★ ★ ★ ★ ★ ★ ★ ★

landscaping – *yard design*

★ ★ ★ ★ ★ ★ ★ ★ ★ ★

Kirk laughed at his father's salesmanship. "Okay. What do I do?" he asked.

The king lost no time showing his son how to help. The two worked all day in the garden. They were so focused on their work that they had to be called in for dinner. After showering and a big meal, they were so tired that they went to bed early. They fell asleep immediately.

The next day they picked up where they'd left off. Kirk was enjoying it so much that he completely forgot about his upcoming speech. The queen mentioned it at dinner that evening.

"Oh," Kirk said, exhaling as though he'd been punched in the stomach.

"You're not ready for your speech?" Luke asked in amusement. His big brother wasn't prepared? He couldn't believe it.

"I, I was wanting help with it when I started working on the garden with Father," Kirk stammered. "But it's no problem. I have the article written. I can just read it!" he said, defending himself.

"Kirk, I'm responsible for distracting you with the gardening. But I'm afraid your plan for the speech isn't acceptable," the king said seriously.

"Why not?" Kirk asked. "My paper has already been approved for the journal. And you said you liked it."

"I do like it. But listening to a paper being read is boring. That's not how to give a good speech." The king paused and studied his children's faces for a moment. "I haven't taught you how to give an informative speech, have I?" he asked. He didn't wait for them to answer. "Follow me to the library," he instructed.

When the royal family arrived in the library, the king withdrew *The Guidebook to Grammar Galaxy* from the shelf. He paged to the article on informative speaking and began reading aloud.

★ ★ ★ ★ ★ ★ ★ ★ ★ ★

anecdotes – *stories*

★ ★ ★ ★ ★ ★ ★ ★ ★ ★

Informative Speaking

A good informative speech begins with a clear outline. Your speech will have an introduction, body, and conclusion.

In most cases, you will want to outline the body of your speech first. Begin by deciding on the three to five main subtopics you will speak about. Under each subtopic, note the key information you will share. Next, plan how to hold your audience's attention for each subtopic. Some common attention-getters to consider are **anecdotes**, jokes, photos, graphs, and demonstrations. Your audience is more likely to remember your attention-getter than your words.

Next, outline your speech's introduction. Begin with an attention-getter that helps your audience understand why your information is important to them. A funny or emotional statistic, quote, or story is a good option. Follow your attention-getter by telling your audience your authority to speak on the subject, even if that's just an interest in the topic. Finally, tell your audience the subtopics you'll be covering in your speech.

The last step in outlining your speech is writing the conclusion. First, you'll review the information you've covered. Then you'll encourage your audience by referring back to your first attention-getter.

See the sample partial outline for a speech on puppy training.

You will cite fewer references in an informative speech. When you do use references for statistics, quotes, or unique ideas, you will give less detail. For example, you might say, "According to the American Kennel Club website, the most important part of puppy training is to start early." Or you might say, "According to a 2013 issue of the *Journal of Veterinary Medical Science*, puppy training is the key to shaping a dog's future behavior."

If your speech requires a title to entice people to listen to you, see "Creating Titles" for help.

After outlining your speech, practice delivering it. The more practice you've had, the more comfortable you will feel. Watch a video of yourself giving the speech and look to see that you're using these tips:

Have occasional eye contact. Look at your audience members, rather than at your notes or over the audience's heads.

Use gestures (movements) that add to your words. Don't fidget with your notes, clothing, or hair.

Smile and remember that your audience wants to hear what you have to say.

The First Simple Commands to Teach Your Puppy

I. Introduction
   A. Many rehomed - behavior problems
   B. Volunteer Humane Society
   C. Happy - how to train, key commands, solve problems

II. Body
   A. How to Train
      1. Attention
      2. Stop the "Squirrel"
   B. Key Commands
      1. Come
      2. Demonstration
   C. Solve Problems
      1. Leave It
      2. Water pistol

III. Conclusion
   A. Learned how to train, key commands, solve problems
   B. Happy; won't have to rehome

"I'm glad I don't have to give an informative speech like Kirk does," Luke joked when his father finished reading.

"Thanks for the idea, Luke," his father said, smirking. "You and the guardians all need to know how to give an informative speech."

Luke groaned.

"I think it will be fun," Ellen said. "We could give speeches in our Grammar Girls and Guys groups."

"Splendid idea, Ellen! Kirk, it would be wonderful if you could give your speech for your Grammar Guys group before the conference," the king said.

Kirk agreed. "I need to get busy then. Luke and Ellen, would you two send out the mission while I work? If I get my speech ready soon, I can get back to helping father in the garden."

Luke and Ellen agreed and worked with their father on a mission called Informative Speaking.

What are *anecdotes*?

What is one tip for delivering a good speech?

Why do you think the king wants Kirk to deliver his speech to the Grammar Guys first?

About the Author

Dr. Melanie Wilson was a clinical psychologist working in a Christian practice, a college instructor, freelance writer, and public speaker before she felt called to stay home and educate her children. She is a mother of six and has homeschooled for 20 years. She says it's her most fulfilling vocation.

Melanie has always been passionate about language arts and used bits and pieces of different curriculum and approaches to teach her children and friends' children. In 2014, she believed she had another calling to write the curriculum she had always wanted as a homeschooling mom — one that didn't take a lot of time, made concepts simple and memorable, and was enough fun to keep her kids motivated.

Books have been a family business since the beginning. Melanie's husband Mark has been selling library books for over 30 years. Melanie and the kids frequently pitch in to help at the annual librarians' conference. Grammar Galaxy is another family business that she hopes will be a great learning opportunity for their children.

When Melanie isn't busy homeschooling, podcasting, or writing, she loves to play tennis with family and friends.

Melanie is also the author of *The Organized Homeschool Life, A Year of Living Productively,* and *So You're Not Wonder Woman.* Learn more on her blog, Psychowith6.com.

About the Illustrator

Rebecca Mueller has had an interest in drawing from an early age. Rebecca quickly developed a unique style and illustrated her first books, a short series of bedtime stories with her mother, at age 9. She has since illustrated for other authors and does graphic design work for several organizations. Rebecca received a BA in English and a minor in Studio Art - Printmaking from the University of Missouri - St. Louis and an honors certificate from the Pierre Laclede Honors College. She is currently working on her Masters in Library Sciences at the University of Missouri - Columbia.

Made in the USA
Columbia, SC
02 January 2021